THE TRUTH ABOUT OUR Families

Loveland, Colorado

The Truth About Our Families
Core Belief Bible Study Series
Copyright © 1998 Group Publishing, Inc.

All rights reserved. No part of this book may be reproduced in any manner whatsoever without prior written permission from the publisher, except where noted in the text and in the case of brief quotations embodied in critical articles and reviews. For information, write Permissions, Group Publishing, Inc., Dept. PD, P.O. Box 481, Loveland, CO 80539.

Credits
Editor: Debbie Gowensmith
Creative Development Editor: Paul Woods
Chief Creative Officer: Joani Schultz
Copy Editor: Betty Taylor
Art Director: Ray Tollison
Cover Art Director: Jeff A. Storm
Computer Graphic Artist/Illustrator: Eris Klein
Photographer: Jafe Parsons
Production Manager: Gingar Kunkel

Unless otherwise noted, Scripture taken from the HOLY BIBLE, NEW INTERNATIONAL VERSION®. Copyright © 1973, 1978, 1984 by International Bible Society. Used by permission of Zondervan Publishing House. All rights reserved.

ISBN 0-7644-0870-4

10 9 8 7 6 5 4 3 2 1   07 06 05 04 03 02 01 00 99 98

Printed in the United States of America.

contents:

the Core Belief: Family

The family has never been more fragile than it is now, and today's kids are painfully aware of that. If they haven't been affected directly by a divorce, they have friends who have. That's why this Core Christian Belief is so important. Today's young people need to learn about God's design for the family.

Kids need to know that God created marriage and the family—he created them before anyone sinned. God created the family because he knew we couldn't bear to live alone. With that in mind, he created us to have spouses and children, brothers and sisters, and everyone else we call family. According to God's Word, the husband-wife relationship should be characterized by mutual love and respect. And the parent-child relationship should be characterized by love, nurture, and spiritual guidance from the parents. In turn, children should respect and obey their parents.

The family shouldn't be a curse. God created it as a blessing.

the Helpful Stuff

FAMILY AS A CORE CHRISTIAN BELIEF **7**
(or Your Home Away From Home)

ABOUT CORE BELIEF BIBLE STUDY SERIES **10**
(or How to Move Mountains in One Hour or Less)

WHY ACTIVE AND INTERACTIVE LEARNING WORKS WITH TEENAGERS **57**
(or How to Keep Your Kids Awake)

YOUR EVALUATION **63**
(or How You Can Edit Our Stuff Without Getting Paid)

the ▼Studies

Blessed Be the Ties... 15
THE ISSUE: Family
THE BIBLE CONNECTION: 1 Corinthians 13:4-7
THE POINT: Family members should love each other.

A Call to Honor 23
THE ISSUE: Honoring Parents
THE BIBLE CONNECTION: Exodus 20:12; 2 Samuel 13:1–18:18; 1 Kings 2:1–4:34; Proverbs 6:20-23; and Ephesians 6:1-3
THE POINT: God wants you to honor your parents.

Rock-a-Bye Baby 35
THE ISSUE: Abortion
THE BIBLE CONNECTION: Genesis 2:18-24; Exodus 21:22-25; Psalms 130:1-4; 139:13-16; Jeremiah 1:4-5; Ephesians 4:29-32; and 1 Timothy 5:3-8
THE POINT: Your family is important to God.

Why Can't We Just Get Along? 45
THE ISSUE: Siblings
THE BIBLE CONNECTION: Genesis 37:17b-28; Numbers 12:1-9; Matthew 5:23-24; 12:46-50; 18:15, 21-22; Luke 10:38-42; Ephesians 4:1-3; Hebrews 13:1; 1 Peter 3:8-9; and 1 John 4:19-21
THE POINT: Your brothers and sisters can be your friends.

Family as a Core Christian Belief

It's a cliché to say that the family is under attack. However, that statement is true today more than ever. Divorce has torn apart the traditional family, making stepfamilies, blended families, and single-parent families more the norm than the exception. If your kids aren't from divorced families, many of their friends most certainly are. As a result, many young people have lost confidence in the family. They don't know whether the families they live in will still be together tomorrow, and they wonder if the families they'll start in a few years will last.

The family is key for the emotional health of generations to come. And if healthy, biblical family relationships are going to make a comeback, today's generation of teenagers may be the key.

Use the studies in this book to help your teenagers understand the importance of family relationships. In the first study, kids will discover that the Bible's message about love applies to their **families.** From the basic message that family members should love each other, students will delve into some specific components of love and learn ways to improve their family relationships.

Next your students will confront their attitudes about **honoring parents.** They'll explore biblical examples of father-son relationships to understand why God wants them to honor their parents.

In the third study, kids will use the Bible to evaluate different opinions about **abortion.** As they study God's Word, they'll discover that their families are important to God.

The last study will help kids learn skills for getting along with their **siblings.** As your students experience empathy, negotiation, teamwork, and appreciation, they'll find that their brothers and sisters can be their friends.

When your young people see and understand God's guidelines for the family, they'll be better equipped to build and maintain positive family relationships that will benefit them for a lifetime.

*For a more comprehensive look at this Core Christian Belief, read Group's **Get Real: Making Core Christian Beliefs Relevant to Teenagers.***

DEPTHFINDER
HOW THE BIBLE DESCRIBES THE FAMILY

To help you effectively guide your kids toward this Core Christian Belief, use these overviews as a launching point for a more in-depth study of the family.

- **The family ideal was established by God in the beginning.** As with many of our Core Christian Beliefs, the family began at Creation. In the Garden of Eden, God made Adam and Eve husband and wife, and thus began the first family. From the beginning, God intended for a man and a woman to forge a lifelong relationship (Genesis 1:27-28; 2:23-25; and Matthew 19:4-6).

- **God created the family to resist isolation.** In the beginning, God declared that it was not good for Adam to be alone, so God created Eve to be Adam's companion. The family should provide love and protection to all, and it should provide guidance and discipline to children (Genesis 2:18-22; 18:19; Deuteronomy 6:4-7; 11:18-21; and Ephesians 5:21–6:4).

- **The husband-wife relationship should be characterized by mutual love and respect.** Maintaining an attitude of love and submission is God's standard for all Christian conduct. This standard also holds true for the marriage relationship. Specifically, the wife is commanded to treat her husband with love and respect. Likewise, the husband is commanded to love his wife as Christ loved the church (1 Corinthians 13:4-7; Ephesians 5:21-33; Colossians 3:18-19; and 1 Peter 3:1-7).

● **Parents should love, nurture, and spiritually guide their children; children should respect and obey their parents.** Since parental love for children most often comes naturally, the Bible gives greater attention to the proper training of children. That training centers on teaching children to follow the guidelines God has laid down for us (Exodus 20:12; Deuteronomy 6:6-9; Proverbs 22:15; 29:15; Ephesians 6:1-4; and Colossians 3:20-21).

CORE CHRISTIAN BELIEF OVERVIEW

Here are the twenty-four Core Christian Belief categories that form the backbone of Core Belief Bible Study Series:

The Nature of God	Jesus Christ
The Holy Spirit	Humanity
Evil	Suffering
Creation	The Spiritual Realm
The Bible	Salvation
Spiritual Growth	Personal Character
God's Justice	Sin & Forgiveness
The Last Days	Love
The Church	Worship
Authority	Prayer
Family	Service
Relationships	Sharing Faith

Look for Group's Core Belief Bible Study Series books in these other Core Christian Beliefs!

about

Bible Study Series
for junior high/middle school

Think for a moment about your young people. When your students walk out of your youth program after they graduate from junior high or high school, what do you want them to know? What foundation do you want them to have so they can make wise choices?

You probably want them to know the essentials of the Christian faith. You want them to base everything they do on the foundational truths of Christianity. Are you meeting this goal?

If you have any doubt that your kids will walk into adulthood knowing and living by the tenets of the Christian faith, then you've picked up the right book. All the books in Group's Core Belief Bible Study Series encourage young people to discover the essentials of Christianity and to put those essentials into practice. Let us explain...

What Is Group's Core Belief Bible Study Series?

Group's Core Belief Bible Study Series is a biblically in-depth study series for junior high and senior high teenagers. This Bible study series utilizes four defining commitments to create each study. These "plumb lines" provide structure and continuity for every activity, study, project, and discussion. They are:

- **A Commitment to Biblical Depth**—Core Belief Bible Study Series is founded on the belief that kids not only *can* understand the deeper truths of the Bible but also *want* to understand them. Therefore, the activities and studies in this series strive to explain the "why" behind every truth we explore. That way, kids learn principles, not just rules.

- **A Commitment to Relevance**—Most kids aren't interested in abstract theories or doctrines about the universe. They want to know how to live successfully right now, today, in the heat of problems they can't ignore. Because of this, each study connects a real-life need with biblical principles that speak directly to that need. This study series finally bridges the gap between Bible truths and the real-world issues kids face.

- **A Commitment to Variety**—Today's young people have been raised in a sound bite world. They demand variety. For that reason, no two meetings in this study series are shaped exactly the same.

- **A Commitment to Active and Interactive Learning**—Active learning is learning by doing. Interactive learning simply takes active learning a step further by having kids teach each other what they've learned. It's a process that helps kids internalize and remember their discoveries.

For a more detailed description of these concepts, see the section titled "Why Active and Interactive Learning Works With Teenagers" beginning on page 57.

So how can you accomplish all this in a set of four easy-to-lead Bible studies? By weaving together various "power" elements to produce a fun experience that leaves kids challenged and encouraged.

- **A Relevant Topic**—More than ever before, kids live in the now. What matters to them and what attracts their hearts is what's happening in their world at this moment. For this reason, every Core Belief Bible Study focuses on a particular hot topic that kids care about.

- **A Core Christian Belief**—Group's Core Belief Bible Study Series organizes the wealth of Christian truth and experience into twenty-four Core Christian Belief categories. These twenty-four headings act as umbrellas for a collection of detailed beliefs that define Christianity and set it apart from the world and every other religion. Each book in this series features one Core Christian Belief with lessons suited for junior high or senior high students.

  "But," you ask, "won't my kids be bored talking about all these spiritual beliefs?" No way! As a youth leader, you know the value of using hot topics to connect with young people. Ultimately teenagers talk about issues because they're searching for meaning in their lives. They want to find the one equation that will make sense of all the confusing events happening around them. Each Core Belief Bible Study answers that need by connecting a hot topic with a powerful Christian principle. Kids walk away from the study with something more solid than just the shifting ebb and flow of their own opinions. They walk away with a deeper understanding of their Christian faith.

- **The Point**—This simple statement is designed to be the intersection between the Core Christian Belief and the hot topic. Everything in the study ultimately focuses on The Point so that kids study it and allow it time to sink into their hearts.

- **The Study at a Glance**—A quick look at this chart will tell you what kids will do, how long it will take them to do it, and what supplies you'll need to get it done.

Helpful Stuff   11

- **The Bible Connection**—This is the power base of each study. Whether it's just one verse or several chapters, The Bible Connection provides the vital link between kids' minds and their hearts. The content of each Core Belief Bible Study reflects the belief that the true power of God—the power to expose, heal, and change kids' lives—is contained in his Word.

THE POINT OF *BETRAYED!*:

God is love.

THE BIBLE CONNECTION

1 JOHN 4:7-21 — The Apostle John explains the nature and definition of perfect love.

In this study, kids will compare the imperfect love defined in real-life stories of betrayal to God's definition of perfect love.

By making this comparison, kids can discover that God is love and therefore incapable of betraying them. Then they'll be able to recognize the incredible opportunity God off relationship worthy of their absolute trust.

Explore the verses in The Bible Connection mation in the Depthfinder boxes throughout understanding of how these Scriptures conne

THE STUDY

DISCUSSION STARTER ▼

Jump-Start (up to 5 minutes) As kids arrive, ask them to thin common themes in movies, books, TV show have kids each contribute ideas for a mast two other kids in the room and sharing t sider providing copies of People maga what's currently showing on television their suggestions, write their respon **come up with a lot of great ide** ent, look through this list and ments most of these themes

After kids make several su responses are connected w

● **Why do you think**

LEADER TIP for The Study Because this topic can be so powerful and relevant to kids' lives, your group members may be tempted to get caught up in issues and lose sight of the deeper biblical principle found in The Point. Help your kids grasp The Point by guiding kids to focus on the biblical investigation and discussing how God's truth connects with reality in their lives.

DEPTHFINDER — UNDERSTANDING INTEGRITY

Your students may not be entirely familiar with the meaning of integrity, especially as it might apply to God's character in the Trinity. Use these definitions (taken from Webster's II New Riverside Dictionary) and other information to help you guide kids toward a better understanding of how God maintains integrity through the three expressions of the Trinity.

Integrity: 1. Firm adherence to a code or standard of values. 2. The state of being unimpaired. 3. The quality or condition of being undivided.

Synonyms for integrity include probity, completeness, wholeness, soundness, and perfection.

Our word "integrity" comes from the Latin word *integritas*, which means soundness. *Integritas* is also the root of the word "integer," which means "whole or complete," as in a "whole" number.

The Hebrew word that's often translated "integrity" (for example, in Psalm 25:21 [NIV]) is *tam*. It means whole, perfect, sincere, and honest.

CREATIVE GOD-EXPLORATION ▼

Top Hats (18 to 20 minutes) Form three groups, with each trio member from the previous activity going to a different group. Give each group Bibles, paper, and pens, and assign each group a different hat God wears: Father, Son, or Holy Spirit.

- **Depthfinder Boxes**—These informative sidelights located throughout each study add insight into a particular passage, word, historical fact, or Christian doctrine. Depthfinder boxes also provide insight into teen culture, adolescent development, current events, and philosophy.

Holy Profiles

Your assigned Bible passage describes how a particular person or group responded when confronted with God's holiness. Use the information in your passage to help your group discuss the questions below. Then use your flashlights to teach the other two groups what you discover.

■ Based on your passage, what does holiness look like?

■ What does holiness sound like?

■ When people see God's holiness, how does it affect them?

■ How is this response to God's holiness like humility?

■ Based on your passage, how would you describe humility?

■ Why is humility an appropriate human response to God's holiness?

■ Based on what you see in your passage, do you think you are a humble person? Why or why not?

■ What's one way you could develop humility in your life this week?

Permission to photocopy this handout from Group's Core Belief Bible Study Series granted for local church use. Copyright © Group Publishing, Inc., Box 481, Loveland, CO 80539.

- **Leader Tips**—These handy information boxes coach you through the study, offering helpful suggestions on everything from altering activities for different-sized groups to streamlining discussions to using effective discipline techniques.

- **Handouts**—Most Core Belief Bible Studies include photocopiable handouts to use with your group. Handouts might take the form of a fun game, a lively discussion starter, or a challenging study page for kids to take home—anything to make your study more meaningful and effective.

The Last Word on Core Belief Bible Studies

Soon after you begin to use Group's Core Belief Bible Study Series, you'll see signs of real growth in your group members. Your kids will gain a deeper understanding of the Bible and of their own Christian faith. They'll see more clearly how a relationship with Jesus affects their daily lives. And they'll grow closer to God.

But that's not all. You'll also see kids grow closer to one another.

That's because this series is founded on the principle that Christian faith grows best in the context of relationship. Each study uses a variety of interactive pairs and small groups and always includes discussion questions that promote deeper relationships. The friendships kids will build through this study series will enable them to grow *together* toward a deeper relationship with God.

THE ISSUE: Family

BLESSED BE the TIES...
How to Really Love Your Family

by Julie Meiklejohn

■ "You *will* clean your room… and I don't want to hear another word about it!" ■ "I don't want to clean my room!" ■ "Do it *now*!" ■ As kids reach adolescence, power struggles within families seem to be the norm rather than the exception. Kids are seeking independence and autonomy from parents, while parents want to protect and nurture their kids. It sometimes seems that kids don't want to have anything to do with their families, but they need their families' love and support. ■ In our families, we should learn, grow, and give and receive unconditional love. But kids may not know what that means. ■ This study will help kids to identify and examine different components of love and how those components fit into their own family relationships. Kids will discover and commit to specific ways they can improve their own relationships with family members.

THE POINT:

Family members should love each other.

The Study
AT A GLANCE

SECTION	MINUTES	WHAT STUDENTS WILL DO	SUPPLIES
Opener	10 to 15	MEET YOUR FAMILY!—Perform family-situation skits with their new "families."	Slips of paper, pencils, two coffee cans
Family Time	25 to 30	LOVE MY FAMILY AS MYSELF?—Travel with their families, explore 1 Corinthians 13:4-7, and apply what they learn to their relationships with family members.	Bibles, "Family—What's Really Important?" handout (p. 22), scissors, tape, newsprint, markers, pencils, paper
Taking It Home	10 to 15	LOVE YOU CAN SEE—Apply what they've learned about expressing love to family members by sharing a special snack and commit to showing love to their own family members.	Ingredients and supplies for banana splits (or another snack), index cards, pencils

notes:

THE POINT OF "BLESSED BE THE TIES...":

Family members should love each other.

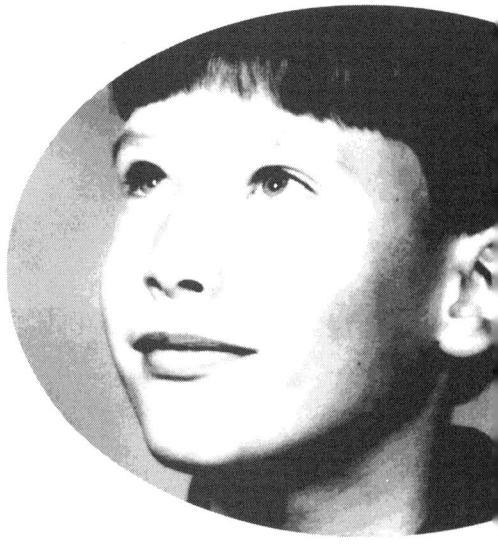

THE BIBLE CONNECTION

1 CORINTHIANS 13:4-7   Paul describes "the most excellent way" of love.

In this study, kids will discover what the Bible says about love and will learn how to apply the components of love to their relationships with family members. Through this experience, kids will find practical ways to demonstrate love to the members of their families.

Explore the verses in The Bible Connection; then study the information in the Depthfinder boxes throughout the study to gain a deeper understanding of how these Scriptures connect with your young people.

BEFORE THE STUDY

For the "Love My Family As Myself?" activity, you'll need to set up three separate stations that are close together enough for minimal travel time but far apart enough for kids to work without distraction. Photocopy the "Family—What's Really Important?" handout (p. 22), and cut apart the three stations. Tape each station's instructions to the floor or a wall at the station. For Station 1, set out several large sheets of newsprint and plenty of markers. For Station 3, set out paper and pencils.

LEADER TIP
for The Study

It's possible that some students in your group may be in negative—even abusive—family situations. The concept of loving members of their families may be very difficult, confusing, and painful. Be sensitive to kids' reactions to this study, and offer to talk privately to any student. Remember that you may have a legal responsibility to report suspected abuse to official authorities. You also may want to read the "Abusive" Depthfinder on page 30.

Blessed Be the Ties...   **17**

THE STUDY

> **LEADER TIP for Meet Your Family!**
>
> In this activity, kids will be forming groups they will "travel" with throughout the rest of the lesson. Groups should have between three and five people, so you'll need to figure out roughly how many people to include in each situation skit group before you start drawing names. You may need to adapt some of the situations to fit the number of people you need in each group.

OPENER ▼

Meet Your Family! (10 to 15 minutes)
As kids arrive, give each person two slips of paper and a pencil. Say: **Today we're going to discuss how family members' treatment of each other can be a blessing. To start, I'd like you to write your name on one of the slips of paper I gave you. On the other slip of paper, write a sentence or two describing a situation that involves a family. It can be either a good situation or a bad situation. For example, you could write about a family arguing over pizza toppings or a family celebrating Thanksgiving together. Make sure your sentences tell who was involved, what happened, where and when it happened, and why you think it happened.** Give kids a few minutes to write, and then have them put the slips with their names on them in one coffee can and the situation slips in the other can.

Say: **Now it's your job to show us some of these situations. I'll draw one of the situations out of the can, and then I'll draw several names out of the other can. The people whose names I draw will form a group, and I'll tell you the role each of you will be playing in the situation. Then groups will have five minutes to create brief skits demonstrating their situations.** Draw names and situations, and then assign roles within each situation. Have kids form groups to prepare their skits.

> **LEADER TIP for Meet Your Family!**
>
> As you draw names and situations, assign each person a role within the family, such as "mom," "dad," "older brother," and so on. You may want to adapt a few situations in order to create a few nontraditional families, such as single-parent families or families that comprise children living with grandparents.

After five minutes, call time, and have groups present their skits. Lead kids in applauding each group's efforts. After groups have finished, have kids answer the following questions within their groups. Have volunteers share their groups' answers with the class. Ask:

● **How do you feel about the way the members of your family treated each other?**

● **Do you think your family members would have treated each other differently if the situation had been a good one** [or a bad one]**?**

● **How should members of any family treat each other?**

● **Should family members treat each other differently depending on the situation they're in? Explain.**

Say: **Today we're going to discuss how family members should treat each other. We're going to discover why <u>family members should love each other</u>, and we're going to find some real, valuable ways we can show love to our family members whatever our situations are. For the rest of the lesson, the people in your skit group will be your "family."**

Blessed Be the Ties... 18

FAMILY TIME ▼

Love My Family As Myself? (25 to 30 minutes)

Say: **For the next part of the lesson, you'll be traveling with your family to three different stations. Follow the instructions at each station, and complete the tasks as a family. In your family, choose one person to be in charge of reading the directions and another person to ensure that everyone is involved in all the tasks at each station. You'll have about twenty-five minutes to complete the three stations. I'll tell you when to switch to another station.** Point out where the stations are located. Assign a fairly even number of groups to each station.

After about seven minutes, have groups move to their next stations. After another seven minutes, have kids move again. After a final seven minutes, have kids come back together in one big group. Say: **You've had a chance to examine what the Bible says about the way people should treat each other. The words of 1 Corinthians 13 can apply especially to families.** Ask:

● **After completing these activities, why do you think family members should love each other?**

● **Is loving family members always easy? Explain.**

● **Why do you think a family's love would be pleasing to God?**

● **What's one thing you learned about how you can show love to your family?**

LEADER TIP for Love My Family As Myself?

You may want to recruit an adult volunteer to help at each station. If you're not able to recruit volunteers, you can tailor the activity to fit the maturity level of your kids. Depending on the size of your group, you may want to complete each station activity together.

LEADER TIP for The Study

Whenever groups discuss a list of questions, write the list on newsprint, and tape it to a wall so groups can discuss the questions at their own pace.

DEPTH FINDER — INVOLVING FAMILIES

One excellent way to help build, preserve, and improve your kids' family relationships is to plan events that involve the whole family. Often, adolescents and their parents have trouble communicating; events that can bring them together on neutral ground while helping them to have fun together may go a long way toward improving family communication. Some ideas for family events include

● a parent-youth retreat,
● a parent-youth "date" night,
● a parent-youth discussion panel,
● a family mission trip,
● youth guest speakers,
● parent guest speakers,
● an "oldies but goodies" night in which parents share their favorite music with their kids,
● seminars for teenagers about getting along with parents,
● seminars for parents about getting along with their kids,
● family game nights,
● family scavenger hunts, and
● family Christmas celebrations.

For more fun ideas that involve the whole family, see *Family-Friendly Ideas Your Church Can Do* (Group Publishing, Inc., 1998).

Blessed Be the Ties... 19

LEADER TIP for The Study

Because this topic can be so powerful and relevant to kids' lives, your group members may be tempted to get caught up in issues and lose sight of the deeper biblical principle found in The Point. Help your kids grasp The Point by guiding them to focus on the biblical investigation and by discussing how God's truth connects with reality in their lives.

TAKING IT HOME ▼

Love You Can See (10 to 15 minutes)

Say: **One of the most important ways we can show love to our family members is by serving them—by trying to see their needs and meeting them without being asked.** Ask:

● **What are some ways you could serve the members of your family?**

Say: **We're going to put this idea into practice with our classroom families now.**

On a large table, set out the ingredients and supplies to make banana splits (or another snack), and explain that one family at a time will go to the table and make banana splits for each other. Say: **You'll need to serve each other—no one can serve himself or herself. One other thing: No one in the family may talk. You'll need to watch one another to determine the needs of your family mem-

---

DEPTH FINDER: THE FAMILY BLESSING

The family blessing is a very important concept that dates back to Old Testament times. In the book of Genesis, we see Jacob "stealing" his father's blessing from his brother Esau. Gaining the blessing was so important that Esau was devastated by the loss. Even today, orthodox Jewish families follow the ancient tradition by bestowing special blessings on their children. The blessings serve to give children a sense of acceptance and protection.

Each member of a family can both bestow and benefit from the tradition of blessing. As outlined in *The Blessing* by Gary Smalley and John Trent, Ph.D., the blessing consists of five important elements:

● **Meaningful touch**—"The act of touch is a key to communicating warmth, personal acceptance, affirmation—even physical health!" How can we show love to the members of our families through touch?

● **A spoken message**—We need to *tell* the people we love how we feel about them. We can't assume that they know. "Good intentions aside, good *words* are necessary to provide genuine acceptance."

● **Attaching high value**—Recognizing a person's amazing worth and value as a child of God is an integral part of blessing. "Words of blessing should carry with them the recognition that this person is valuable and has redeeming qualities. In the Scriptures, recognition is based on who they are, not simply on their performance."

● **Picturing a special future**—While we cannot picture other people's futures, we can "encourage and help them to set meaningful goals," as well as convey to them that "the gifts and character traits they have right now are attributes that God can bless and use in the future."

● **An active commitment**—This is the confirmation of the blessing and entails a great deal of responsibility. "Words alone cannot communicate the blessing; they need to be backed with a commitment to do everything possible to help the one blessed be successful."

How can we use these elements to bless the people we love?

Permission to photocopy this Depthfinder from Group's Core Belief Bible Study Series granted for local church use. Copyright © Group Publishing, Inc., P.O. Box 481, Loveland, CO 80539.

DEPTHFINDER: EXPLORING THE BIBLE

Another passage in the Bible that explores God's will for family members is Ephesians 5:21–6:4. The passage asks us to examine the nature of the church's submission to Christ and asks each person to "submit to one another out of reverence for Christ." Rather than a submission that is enforced by means of tradition, it is a submission that is "freely assumed in humble response to [Christ's] self-giving, sacrificial servanthood and his continuing empowerment and nurturing presence" (Walter C. Kaiser Jr. et al., *Hard Sayings of the Bible*).

By applying this idea to family relationships, we see that God desires each family member to submit to the other family members. We are asked to give freely of ourselves, to serve each other, and to nurture and support each other, just as the church does as Christ's body.

In 1 Corinthians 13, Paul provided a detailed breakdown of what such submission looks like in practice. By being conscious of and working to embody the qualities described in 1 Corinthians 13 in our own familial relationships, we can further strengthen the entire body of Christ within the world.

LEADER TIP for The Study

This would be a great study in which to get your teenagers' family members involved! Involving family members creates shared experiences and is a great way to open or improve communication. If you decide to invite family members, encourage them to participate fully in all of the activities.

bers. I'll tell each family when to get the snack. After you have your snack, you may sit back down with your family and enjoy it!

Hand out index cards and pencils, and say: **While one family's members are serving each other, I'd like the rest of you to think about the different ways that we talked about today of showing love to family members. Choose one way of showing love that you feel you can commit to during this week, and write it on your card. For example, you might write, "I'll show love by helping my little brother with his homework" or "I'll show love by not arguing with my mom when she asks me to do something."**

Have one family at a time make snacks for each other until all the groups have eaten their snacks. Then say: **Today we've examined why <u>family members should love each other</u>, and we've discussed practical ways to show love to our family members. I'd like us to close in prayer. I'll begin the prayer, and then we'll have a few moments of silence in which you can ask God to help you keep the commitment you wrote down. Then I'll close the prayer.** Begin the prayer by saying: **Dear God, thank you for families. Please help us to show love to our family members...** Allow a few moments for kids to pray in silence, and then close the prayer.

You may want to give kids photocopies of the "Family Blessing" Depthfinder (p. 20) to help them discover more meaningful ways to show love to their families.

Remind kids to take their commitment cards home with them.

FAMILY — *What's Really Important?*

STATION 1

As a group, read 1 Corinthians 13:4 and then follow the instructions below.

1. Take turns answering these questions in your group:
   - Which characteristic in this verse do you find easiest to practice with your family members?
   - Which characteristic do you find most difficult?

2. As a group, choose one of the characteristics. Use the newsprint and markers to create a banner that shows (or tells) ways you can use the characteristic to show love to your own family members. Make sure that everyone's ideas are included and that everyone has a part in creating the banner. Keep your completed banner with you.

At the leader's instruction, move to Station 2. Be sure to leave this sheet here.

STATION 2

As a group, read 1 Corinthians 13:5, and then follow the instructions below.

1. Take turns sharing about a family situation in which you had a difficult time with one of the characteristics in this verse. For example, you might tell about a time you got really mad at your brother because he got to watch what he wanted to on TV.

2. Take turns completing the following sentences within your group:
   - I get angry at a member of my family when…
   - When I get angry, I act…
   - To express love instead of anger at a family member, I could…

3. Brainstorm together other ways to finish the previous sentence.

At the leader's instruction, move to Station 3. Be sure to leave this sheet here.

STATION 3

As a group, read 1 Corinthians 13:6-7, and then follow the instructions below.

1. Take turns answering this question:
   - Which of the characteristics in these verses seem to be most important in helping you love your family. Why?

2. Form pairs (or trios). In your pairs, take turns interviewing each other using the following questions. The interviewer needs to write down the answers.
   - Think of a person in your family who demonstrates one of these characteristics. Who are you thinking of, and what characteristic does that person demonstrate?
   - What does that person do to demonstrate that characteristic to the rest of the family?
   - What could you do to be more like that person?

3. Share with the rest of your family group some of the responses to the questions.

At the leader's instruction, move to Station 1. Be sure to leave this sheet here.

Permission to photocopy this handout from Group's Core Belief Bible Study Series granted for local church use.
Copyright © Group Publishing, Inc., P.O. Box 481, Loveland, CO 80539.

THE ISSUE: Honoring Parents

A CALL TO HONOR

by Michael D. Warden

■ What would you do if your brother had raped your little sister—and your father chose to do nothing about it? Or what if your father ignored you for five years? How would you respond? How would you "honor" your father in a situation like that? ■ That was the life Absalom lived under his father, David. Absalom went on to lead a rebellion against his father, toward whom he no doubt felt resentment. We might criticize Absalom's choices now, but how many of us would have acted differently if we had been in his shoes? ■ Honoring parents can be difficult, especially when they do things that hurt us. But God wants all of us to honor our parents regardless of what they do. Even though your students are young and their parents are certainly far from perfect, God expects children to honor their parents. ■ This study guides kids on an exploration of two brothers, Absalom and Solomon, and compares how well each son honored his parents—even when his parents didn't honor him in return. ■ Use this study to help kids discover practical ways to honor their parents—regardless of how their parents treat them.

Why Kids Should Honor Their Parents— **NO MATTER WHAT!**

THE POINT:

God wants you to honor your parents.

The Study AT A GLANCE

SECTION	MINUTES	WHAT STUDENTS WILL DO	SUPPLIES
Brain Teaser	5 to 10	HONOR SOUP—Use Scripture to help create an assortment of definitions of "honor" and then merge them into one.	Bibles, tape, newsprint, markers, paper, pens
Creative Drama	20 to 25	A PRESENTATION OF HONOR—Prepare and present two skits that illustrate how Absalom and Solomon treated their parents.	"Absalom" skit (pp. 32-33), "Solomon" skit (p. 34)
In-Depth Investigation	5 to 10	A TEST OF HONOR—Use the definition they created to evaluate how well Absalom and Solomon honored their parents.	Bibles, paper, pens, kids' definition of honor from "Honor Soup" activity, newsprint, tape, marker
	10 to 15	MY PERSONAL HONOR—Evaluate how well they honored their parents in the past week.	Bibles, paper, pens, kids' definition of honor from "Honor Soup" activity
Life Application	up to 5	HONOR ADJUSTMENT—With partners, commit to honoring their parents in specific ways in the coming week.	Paper, pens

notes:

THE POINT OF "A CALL TO HONOR":

God wants you to honor your parents.

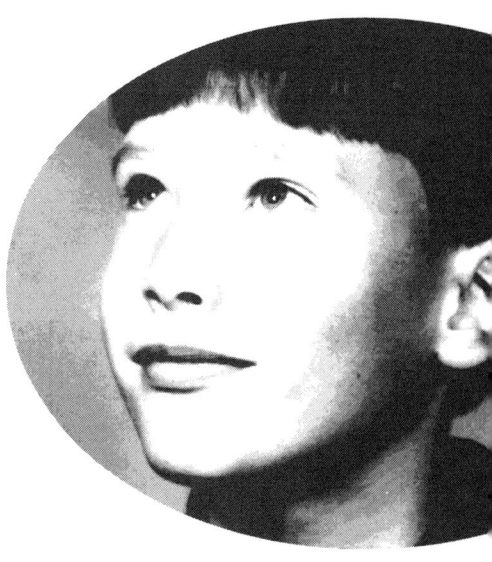

THE BIBLE CONNECTION

EXODUS 20:12	God commands his people to honor their parents.
2 SAMUEL 13:1–18:18	The author chronicles Absalom's relationship with his family.
1 KINGS 2:1–4:34	The author chronicles Solomon's relationship with his parents.
PROVERBS 6:20-23	Solomon offers advice on the importance of obeying parents.
EPHESIANS 6:1-3	Paul instructs Christians to honor and obey their parents.

In this study, kids will create a biblical definition of "honor" and then will use dramatic presentations to evaluate how well Absalom and Solomon honored their parents. Then kids will create personal time lines and evaluate how well they honor their own parents.

Through these creative evaluations, kids can discover why God thinks it's important for them to honor their parents and can find simple, practical ways to honor their parents more effectively.

Explore the verses in The Bible Connection; then examine the information in the Depthfinder boxes throughout the study to gain a deeper understanding of how these Scriptures connect with your young people.

BEFORE THE STUDY

For the "Presentation of Honor" activity, photocopy the "Absalom" skit (pp. 32-33) and the "Solomon" skit (p. 34).

LEADER TIP for The Study

Some of your kids' parents may be divorced, absent, alcoholic, or addicted to drugs. A few of them may even be abusive. As you talk about the importance of honoring parents, be sensitive to kids who are in situations like these. Let kids know that you realize not every home is perfect and that honoring parents can be very challenging. Offer to talk privately with anyone who wants to. If a student talks about abuse taking place in his or her family, tell your pastor immediately. Remember that you may have a legal responsibility to report suspected abuse to official authorities.

A Call to Honor

THE STUDY

LEADER TIP for The Study

Whenever groups discuss a list of questions, write the list on newsprint and tape it to a wall so groups can discuss the questions at their own pace.

LEADER TIP for Honor Soup

If you have more than ten students, have kids form groups of six or fewer so each group can create its own megadefinition of honor. Then bring the whole class back together for the discussion.

LEADER TIP for Honor Soup

If your students come up with definition ideas for honor that may not correspond with the Bible, ask kids to explain how they got their ideas from the passages you assigned. Then, to help keep kids on track, read aloud the biblical definition for honor provided in the Depthfinder on page 27.

BRAIN TEASER ▼

Honor Soup (5 to 10 minutes)

As kids arrive, tape a sheet of newsprint to a wall, and write "honor" across the top. Then write the following Bible references: Exodus 20:12; Proverbs 6:20-23; and Ephesians 6:1-3. Have kids form pairs, and then give each pair a Bible, a sheet of paper, and a pen. Say: **Read the passages I've listed on the newsprint; then, based on those passages, write a definition of the word "honor" on your paper. Start your definition by writing, "To honor people means to," and then complete the sentence.**

After a couple of minutes, gather kids together. Have one pair write its definition on the newsprint. Then have a second pair add its definition to the first one. For example, if the first pair writes, "To honor people means to treat them with respect," the second pair could add, "never lie to them." Continue this process until each pair has added its definition.

You should end up with one long, detailed definition—for example, "To honor people means to treat them with respect, never lie to them, help them, obey them, listen to them, remember what they tell you, let them teach you, and don't think of yourself more highly than them."

Once the megadefinition is complete, allow kids to make any changes they want—editing questionable phrases or merging redundant ideas—until they come up with a detailed, biblical definition of honor.

Then ask:

● **Was it hard for you to merge your definition with all the other definitions? Why or why not?**

● **How is merging our definitions together like this a way of honoring each other's perspective?**

● **Would you like to be honored in the way this definition describes? Why or why not?**

● **Who should we honor in the way this definition describes? Why?**

● **Who do you have the most trouble honoring in the way this definition describes? Explain.**

Say: **For a lot of us, it is not hardest to honor teachers or pastors or government leaders—it's hardest to honor our parents. That's because by now we've all learned that none of our parents is perfect—and some might even be considered "bad." But today we're going to talk about why <u>God wants you to honor your parents</u> regardless of whether you think they're good or bad. We'll investigate how some young people in the Bible honored (or didn't honor) their parents, and we'll evaluate how well we honor our own parents based on the definition you've just created.**

A Call to Honor 26

CREATIVE DRAMA ▼

A Presentation of Honor (20 to 25 minutes)

Have kids form two groups. Give one group a copy of the "Absalom" skit (pp. 32-33), and give the other group a copy of the "Solomon" skit (p. 34). Assign kids the various roles, or let kids choose the roles for themselves. If you have more students than parts, extra students may act as the optional players listed in the skits.

After all the parts are assigned, have groups read their assigned skits to familiarize themselves with the stories. Then say: **We're going to do these skits as impromptu performances. Just act out whatever the Narrators say, and ham it up as much as you like. As the skits are presented, think about how well Absalom and Solomon measured up to our definition of honor in the way they treated their parents. Through these examples, we want to find out why <u>God wants you to honor your parents</u>.**

Have groups take turns presenting their skits to the rest of the class. Applaud groups' efforts, and congratulate them on their spontaneous creativity. Then have kids form groups of four to discuss these questions:

● What's your reaction to the story of Absalom? of Solomon?
● Do you think Absalom got what he deserved? Why or why not?
● Did Solomon get what he deserved? Why or why not?
● Would you consider King David a good father? Explain.
● If you were David, what would you have done differently as a father?
● What would you have done differently if you were Absalom? Solomon?

LEADER TIP for A Presentation of Honor

If you have more than twenty-five students, have kids form four groups instead of two; then have each group perform its own version of either the "Absalom" or "Solomon" skit.

If you have fewer than fifteen students, have kids play multiple parts in the skits. To help kids separate their characters, give them props to use with each character. For example, a broomstick "spear" could be a prop for Absalom, while a hat could be a "crown" for King David. Have kids switch props depending on which character they're portraying.

DEPTH FINDER — UNDERSTANDING THE BIBLE

Because the English word "honor" has been translated from several different Hebrew and Greek words, it's helpful to look at how the Hebrew and Greek words for "honor" have been used in other verses. Such a comparison reveals that "honor" in Exodus 20:12 means to prize highly, to care and show affection, and to show respect and reverence.

Proverbs 6:20-23 helps us to see *why* we should honor our parents. We are to listen to and obey what our parents teach us, and what they teach will protect us and give us direction.

When Paul speaks to children in Ephesians 6:1-3, he reminds us that we're to value our parents. The Greek for "obey your parents" tells us that "obedience on the part of children consists in listening to the advice given by parents." In quoting God's command to honor parents in Ephesians 6:2, Paul uses the Greek word *tima*, which means more than simply to obey. It is to respect and esteem.

Use this information to help kids create a more accurate definition of honor for this study.

(Source: Frank E. Gœbelein, *The Expositor's Bible Commentary*)

A Call to Honor

LEADER TIP for The Study

Because this topic can be so powerful and relevant to kids' lives, your group members may be tempted to get caught up in issues and lose sight of the deeper biblical principle found in The Point. Help your kids grasp The Point by guiding them to focus on the biblical investigation and by discussing how God's truth connects with reality in their lives.

● What do these stories teach us about honoring our parents?

Say: <u>God wants you to honor your parents</u>. And stories like the ones we just heard are included in the Bible so we can learn what "honoring our parents" really means. Now that we know something about the family life of these two brothers, let's take a closer look at how they did—or did not—honor their parents through their choices.

IN-DEPTH INVESTIGATION ▼

A Test of Honor (5 to 10 minutes) Have kids stay in their groups, and give each group paper, pens, and a Bible. Point to the definition of honor kids created in the first activity, and say: **This is the measuring rod we've decided to use to determine whether these brothers honored their parents. Think about the skit you presented and the skit you watched. Using this definition, rate how well each brother honored his parents. On your paper, write two scores—one for Absalom and one for Solomon. You may want to look up parts of the stories to help you decide. Use a rating scale from one to ten, with ten being absolute perfection and one being utter failure. For example, if you think one brother did most things right but messed up in a few areas, you might rate him at seven or eight. But, hey, you're the judge. You make the call. We'll talk about your scores in a few minutes.**

Tell kids that everyone must participate by offering a score for both Absalom and Solomon. Explain that to come up with a final score for each brother, each group should average its group members' scores.

DEPTHFINDER — **TEN GREAT WAYS FOR KIDS TO HONOR THEIR PARENTS**

1. Say, "Thank you" often.
2. Tell them how your day went—using more than five words.
3. Clean up the kitchen, take out the trash, mow the lawn, or do other household chores—without being asked.
4. Be nice to your siblings.
5. Ask permission before inviting friends over or going somewhere with friends.
6. Ask your parents for advice—even if it's about little things like which toothpaste you should use.
7. When you do something wrong, admit it and ask for forgiveness.
8. Speak highly of them when they're not around.
9. Say, "I love you" often.
10. When you don't know what else to do, hug them.

Permission to photocopy this Depthfinder from Group's Core Belief Bible Study Series granted for local church use. Copyright © Group Publishing, Inc., P.O. Box 481, Loveland, CO 80539.

A Call to Honor 28

For example, if one group's members rate Absalom at 3, 5, 5, and 6, the average is almost 5.

To help groups decide how to rate each brother, encourage them to think about what each brother did (did his actions honor his parents?); what motivated each brother's actions (did he *try* to honor his parents even if it didn't work out the way he wanted?); and what other people said or wrote about each brother's actions (did other people think he honored his parents?).

While groups decide their scores, tape a sheet of newsprint to a wall. At the top, write, "Honor Score." Then draw a line down the center of the newsprint. On one side write, "Absalom," and on the other write, "Solomon."

When groups are ready, have them present their scores. Write each group's scores on the newsprint. Then ask:
● **Why did you rate Absalom the way you did?**
● **According to our definition of honor, what do you think Absalom should have done differently to honor his parents?**
● **Why did you rate Solomon the way you did?**
● **According to our definition, what do you think Solomon should have done differently to honor his parents?**
● **How might the skit have been different if Absalom or Solomon had honored his parents in the way you suggest?**
● **Why should Absalom and Solomon have cared whether they honored their parents?**
● **Why do you think <u>God wants you to honor your parents</u>?**

My Personal Honor (10 to 15 minutes)

Say: **Evaluating how well Absalom and Solomon honored their parents is helpful. But the Bible teaches that <u>God wants you to honor your parents</u>, too. So now let's make it personal.**

Have each person find a partner from a different group. Distribute paper and pens, and then have pairs discuss these questions:
● **What would you have said to Absalom if he had asked you for advice before doing anything the skit described?**
● **What would you have said to Solomon?**
● **Which brother is most like you? Explain.**
● **Do you think it's important for you to honor your parents? Why or why not?**
● **What makes it hard for you to honor your parents?**

Say: **On your paper, create a time line of any interaction you've had with your parents in the past week. For example, make a note of every time you ate together, did something else together, or talked about anything. When you're finished, explain your time line to your partner.**

When kids have finished explaining their time lines to their partners, point to the definition of honor and say: **Now it gets tough. Using this definition, rate yourself according to how well you honored**

LEADER TIP for My Personal Honor

To help kids create their time lines, you might want to write a sample time line on a sheet of newsprint. Here's an example:
Sunday—Went to church with parents. Didn't talk about anything.
Monday—Mom made me dinner. I ate it in my room so I could play video games.
Tuesday—Talked to Mom a little in the morning.
Wednesday—Mom and Dad got mad at me about a grade on an English quiz.
Thursday—Nothing happened.
Friday—Parents went out to dinner. I stayed home and talked on the phone.
Saturday—Mom and Dad made me do some work around the house. Left to go to a friend's house as soon as I was finished. Watched television with parents for a while on Saturday night.

A Call to Honor

your parents during the past week. Use the same approach you used with Absalom and Solomon. Write your personal score on the back of your time line.

When kids finish, have them share their scores with their partners. Then have pairs discuss these questions:
● **How do you feel about your score? Explain.**
● **Why did you rate yourself the way you did?**
● **Read Proverbs 6:20-23. Do you think Solomon's advice in this passage is true for your family? Why or why not?**
● **What makes it hard for you to honor your parents in the way our definition describes?**

DEPTHFINDER: HONORING AN ABUSIVE PARENT

Some of your students may be victims of parents who abuse them verbally, physically, or sexually. Abuse in any form is a serious problem and should not be taken lightly. If students make comments during the study that cause you to suspect abuse, talk to them privately about their situations at home. Don't pressure students for information, and don't ask leading questions. Just listen closely to what your students say to make sure you understand what they're telling you. For example, a student who says he feels "beat up" at home may not mean to imply that his parents beat him. He just may be using a figure of speech.

After talking with students, if you believe abuse may be occurring, immediately notify your pastor. Remember that you may have a legal responsibility to report suspected abuse to official authorities. Your church most likely has information on local counseling agencies that can help abusive families change their behavior.

If you want more information on how to deal with abuse in families, contact one or more of these agencies:

● Childhelp USA, Inc.
6463 Independence Ave.
Woodland Hills, CA 91367
1-800-422-4453

● Incest Survivors Anonymous
P.O. Box 5613
Long Beach, CA 90800

● The Minirth-Meier Clinic West (a Christian mental health services agency)
1-800-545-1819

● National Association for Children of Alcoholics
31582 Coast Highway, Suite B
South Laguna, CA 92677
(714) 499-3889

● National Council on Child Abuse and Family Violence
1155 Connecticut Ave. N.W., Suite 400
Washington, D.C. 20036
1-800-222-2000

- **What advice can you offer yourself on how you can improve your score?**
- **What advice can you offer your partner on how he or she can improve his or her score?**

After the discussion, say: <u>**God wants you to honor your parents**</u>, **but it won't always be easy. By praying for God's strength and wisdom, we can learn to honor our parents in ways that please God—even when our parents aren't perfect.**

LIFE APPLICATION ▼

Honor Adjustment (up to 5 minutes) Have kids stay in pairs. Based on the definition of honor and all they've discussed, have kids each think of two practical things they can do in the coming week to honor their parents. For example, kids might decide to ask their parents about their day, offer to help clean the kitchen, or do their homework without being asked. Have kids write their ideas on their papers underneath their scores and share what they wrote with their partners. Then have partners pray together, asking God to give them the strength and wisdom to honor their parents.

Then say: <u>**God wants you to honor your parents**</u>. **And we can help each other accomplish that goal. On your own sheet, copy the two ideas your partner came up with. Commit to pray for your partner at least once this week, asking God to help your partner honor his or her parents this week. Then sometime next week, ask your partner how the week went. You'll be surprised how much things can change with just a little effort.**

Direct kids to the definition of honor one more time. Say: **For our closing, look over this definition, and tell your partner one aspect of this definition you already see in his or her life. For example, you might say, "You're always honest" or "You're a good listener."**

When pairs have finished, dismiss the class. Encourage them to take home their time lines as reminders to honor their parents in the coming week.

LEADER TIP for Honor Adjustment

To help kids come up with practical ideas for honoring their parents, photocopy the "Ten Great Ways for Kids to Honor Their Parents" Depthfinder (p. 28), and give each person a copy.

A Call to Honor

Absalom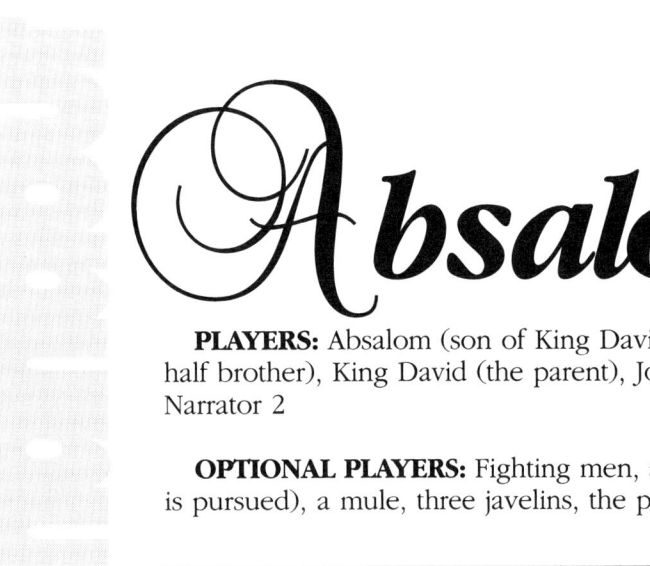

BASED ON 2 SAMUEL 13:1–18:18

PLAYERS: Absalom (son of King David), Tamar (Absalom's sister), Amnon (Absalom's half brother), King David (the parent), Joab (David's military leader), Narrator 1, and Narrator 2

OPTIONAL PLAYERS: Fighting men, a large oak tree, horses (for whoever pursues or is pursued), a mule, three javelins, the people

---

NARRATOR 1: This is the story of Absalom (AB-sah-lum) and King David that is based on 2 Samuel 13:1–18:18. Absalom was very close to his sister Tamar (TAY-mahr). They liked hanging out together and shooting the breeze. But they had a half brother, Amnon (AM-non), who was a real social deviant. He did something that really hurt Tamar—so much that she wanted to die. When Tamar told Absalom what Amnon had done, Absalom went berserk! King David also heard about what happened, and he went berserk too! But King David never did anything about the situation. He just turned a blind eye to the whole thing.

NARRATOR 2: Absalom, however, did do something. After plotting and scheming for two years, he came up with a shrewd idea. He threw a huge party and invited all the king's sons, including Amnon. The party was really jammin', and Amnon was having a good time and drinking a lot of wine. After Amnon got really drunk, Absalom had his men kill Amnon. So he avenged what Amnon had done to his sister Tamar.

NARRATOR 1: When King David heard about Amnon's murder, he went berserk again! Absalom was scared about what the king might do, so he ran away and hid. Once again, though, King David did nothing about the situation. He didn't try to talk to Absalom or ask him to come back home; he didn't even punish Absalom. The king just sat and moped around the palace. So Absalom stayed away for three years. And even though King David longed to see Absalom, he did nothing.

NARRATOR 2: King David's military leader, Joab (JO-ab), got really tired of David's moping around all the time. Finally Joab helped David to realize that Absalom should come home, and David sent Joab to bring Absalom home. When Absalom returned to the city, though, David refused to see him. David told Joab to tell Absalom that he was not allowed to come to the palace or see the king for any reason. So Absalom was really upset.

Permission to photocopy this handout from Group's Core Belief Bible Study Series granted for local church use.
Copyright © Group Publishing, Inc., P.O. Box 481, Loveland, CO 80539.

NARRATOR 1: For two years, Absalom was not allowed to see the king or go to the palace. Finally Absalom couldn't take it anymore. He told his men to set Joab's fields on fire. When Joab asked Absalom about the fire, Absalom demanded to see his father. King David gave in and agreed to see Absalom. When they met, they hugged and made up—or so it seemed. But really, Absalom was very angry about what his father had done. So Absalom plotted a rebellion against the king.

NARRATOR 2: Absalom began telling the people, "If I were king, things would be different. I would be a better king than my father, David." After years of this, Absalom asked his men to fight with him to overthrow the king. The men agreed. When the king heard about the rebellion, he and almost everyone at the palace ran away together. So Absalom declared himself king in his father's place.

NARRATOR 1: King David gathered his own men and asked them to fight Absalom's men. But David told his men not to harm Absalom even though he had overthrown David's kingdom. Joab led David's fighting men out to find Absalom's army. By chance, one of David's men saw Absalom. Absalom had been riding a mule, but he had ridden under a large oak tree, and his long hair had gotten tangled in the branches. The branches had pulled Absalom off his donkey and had left him dangling in the tree. David's fighting men refused to kill Absalom because of the king's order. But when Joab saw Absalom, he speared three javelins through Absalom's heart.

NARRATOR 2: Then David's men took Absalom out of the tree and buried him in the forest under a pile of rocks.

Solomon son of King David
Based on 1 Kings 2:1–4:34

PLAYERS: Solomon (son of King David, Benaiah (Solomon's military leader), Joab (David's military leader), Shimei (an enemy of King David's), King David (the parent), God, Narrator 1, and Narrator 2

OPTIONAL PLAYERS: Fighting men, the altar, two slaves, a donkey

NARRATOR 1: This is the story of Solomon and David that is based on 1 Kings 2:1–4:34. Solomon was not King David's oldest son, but David had decided to make Solomon king after him, anyway. So when King David was on his deathbed, he called Solomon to him to give a few last-minute instructions.

NARRATOR 2: King David asked Solomon to clear up some of David's unfinished business and to prevent civil war. For example, David asked Solomon to have Joab (JO-ab) killed because Joab had killed people he shouldn't have killed. David also asked Solomon to keep an eye on a fellow named Shimei (SHIM-ee-i). That's because Shimei had sided with Absalom (AB-sah-lum) during the rebellion and had actually thrown rocks on David's head as he fled Jerusalem. After David had said these things, he died.

NARRATOR 1: As king, Solomon started to fulfill his father's requests. When Joab heard that King Solomon might be out to get him, he ran to the tent of the Lord and took hold of the altar, clinging to it like a baby to his mother. Solomon heard that Joab was there, so he sent Benaiah (bee-NAY-uh) to kill him. Benaiah tried to get Joab to come away from the altar, but he refused. After consulting with King Solomon again, Benaiah killed him anyway—right there by the altar.

NARRATOR 2: Next King Solomon summoned Shimei and said to him, "I've decided not to kill you for what you did to my father. But I command you to stay in Jerusalem where I can keep an eye on you for as long as you live. The day you leave Jerusalem will be the day you die." Shimei agreed to the king's terms and stayed in Jerusalem for three years. But then...

NARRATOR 1: Two of Shimei's slaves escaped, so Shimei saddled his donkey and went to fetch them. By the time he had returned to Jerusalem, King Solomon had heard that Shimei had left town. So the king called Shimei before him and asked, "Why did you not keep your oath to the Lord and obey me?" Then Solomon asked Benaiah to kill Shimei. And Benaiah did.

NARRATOR 2: After Solomon had fulfilled his father's requests, the Lord appeared to Solomon in a dream. God told Solomon to ask for whatever he wanted God to give to him. Solomon said to God, "You have been faithful to my father David because he was righteous and upright in heart. Now you've made me king in his place. But I am too young to know how to rule well. So give me wisdom and discernment so I can govern your people well."

NARRATOR 1: God was really pleased with Solomon's request. So he said, "Because you asked for this instead of wealth, long life, or victory over your enemies, I will not only grant your request, but I will also give you all the things you didn't ask for. I will give you riches and honor above all other kings during your lifetime. And if you obey me as your father did, I will give you a long life."

NARRATOR 2: Solomon went on to become the wisest man who ever lived. He spoke three thousand proverbs; wrote more than one thousand songs; and studied plant life, animals, birds, reptiles, and fish. The people came from all around to benefit from Solomon's wisdom. And he lived a long, peaceful life.

Permission to photocopy this handout from Group's Core Belief Bible Study Series granted for local church use.
Copyright © Group Publishing, Inc., P.O. Box 481, Loveland, CO 80539.

THE ISSUE: Abortion

Rock-a-Bye Baby

Helping Kids Seek God's View on Abortion

by Lisa Baba Lauffer

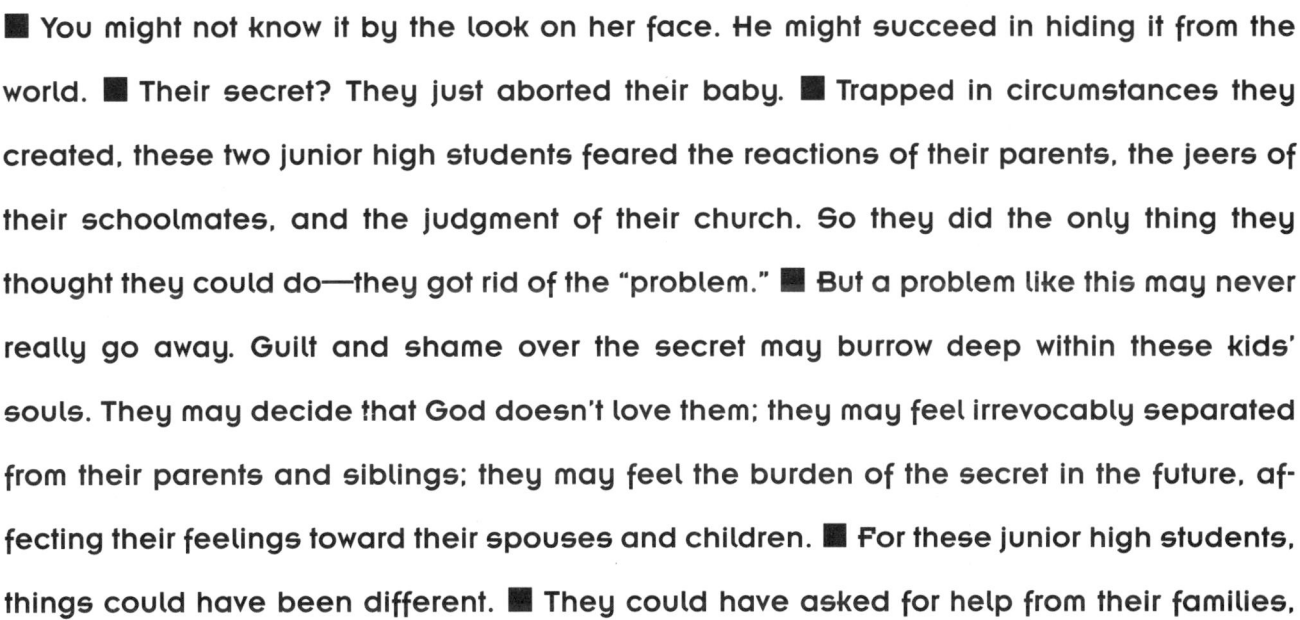

■ You might not know it by the look on her face. He might succeed in hiding it from the world. ■ Their secret? They just aborted their baby. ■ Trapped in circumstances they created, these two junior high students feared the reactions of their parents, the jeers of their schoolmates, and the judgment of their church. So they did the only thing they thought they could do—they got rid of the "problem." ■ But a problem like this may never really go away. Guilt and shame over the secret may burrow deep within these kids' souls. They may decide that God doesn't love them; they may feel irrevocably separated from their parents and siblings; they may feel the burden of the secret in the future, affecting their feelings toward their spouses and children. ■ For these junior high students, things could have been different. ■ They could have asked for help from their families, from their church, and from God. If they had, they could have learned that they're loved and forgiven. ■ In this study, kids will think about the issues surrounding abortion. The study encourages an open, safe discussion so kids can feel confident that their families—and everything that affects them—are important to God.

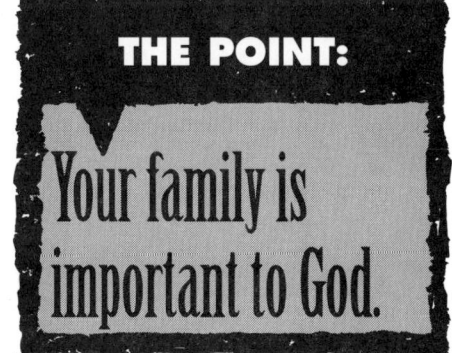

THE POINT:

Your family is important to God.

The Study
AT A GLANCE

SECTION	MINUTES	WHAT STUDENTS WILL DO	SUPPLIES
Opening Experience	up to 5	BEAN TRAUMA—Try to destroy a bean buried in dirt without spilling any dirt.	Pinto beans, paper cups, soil
Creative Discussion	20 to 25	ANONYMOUS DEBATE—Debate the issues surrounding abortion from a random viewpoint.	Masking tape, newsprint, markers, index cards, pencils, a paper bag, "Questions List" handouts (p. 44)
Bible Exploration	15 to 20	SEEKING GOD'S VIEW—Explore various Bible passages to look for God's view of abortion and the family.	Bibles, paper, pencils, opinion areas from previous activity
Response and Commitment	10 to 15	TRUE STORIES—Respond to teenage girls' comments about abortion.	Paper, pencils

notes:

THE POINT OF "ROCK-A-BYE BABY":

Your family is important to God.

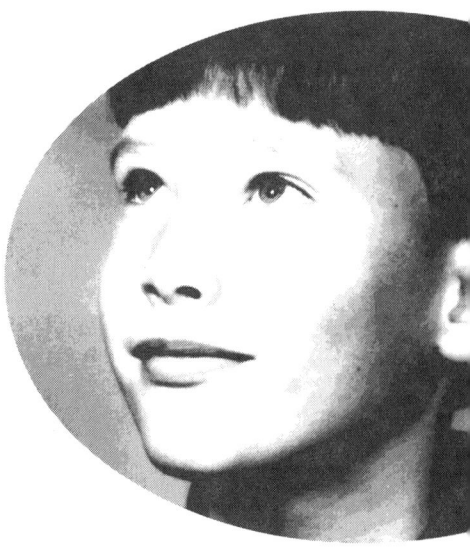

THE BIBLE CONNECTION

GENESIS 2:18-24	God creates family as a blessing.
EXODUS 21:22-25	God's law to Israel demands payment for injuries to pregnant women or their unborn babies.
PSALM 130:1-4	God forgives.
PSALM 139:13-16	David praises God for creating him and knowing him before he was born.
JEREMIAH 1:4-5	God knew Jeremiah before he was born.
EPHESIANS 4:29-32	Christians should build each other up and treat each other with love.
1 TIMOTHY 5:3-8	Paul asks Christians to take care of their family members.

In this study, kids will creatively debate the issue of abortion and then will look in the Bible for guidance relating to abortion and for the importance God places on the family.

Through this experience, kids can determine their own views on abortion and can learn that decisions that affect their families are important to God.

Explore the verses in The Bible Connection; then examine the information in the Depthfinder boxes throughout the study to gain a deeper understanding of how these Scriptures connect with your young people.

BEFORE THE STUDY

For the "Bean Trauma" activity, fill paper cups to the top with soil, and bury one pinto bean in each cup. Prepare one cup for each student.

For the "Anonymous Debate" activity, write each of the five opinion headings from the "Questions List" handout (p. 44) across the top of a separate sheet of newsprint. Then use masking tape to divide your meeting room into five equal pie-shaped sections. Tape one of the prepared sheets of newsprint to the wall of each section. Also, make enough photocopies of the "Questions List" handout for every student to have one.

LEADER TIP for The Study

Because this study deals with such a sensitive, controversial topic, you may want to talk with students' parents at least a few days before the study. Let parents know that the study presents differing opinions about abortion. Parents will appreciate your openness, and they'll be prepared to talk with their kids at home about their own views concerning abortion.

Rock-a-Bye Baby 37

LEADER TIP for The Study

You may want to invite your pastor to class to talk about your church's position concerning abortion.

LEADER TIP for The Study

Because this topic can be so powerful and relevant to kids' lives, your group members may be tempted to get caught up in issues and lose sight of the deeper biblical principle found in The Point. Help your kids grasp The Point by guiding them to focus on the biblical investigation and by discussing how God's truth connects with reality in their lives.

THE STUDY

OPENING EXPERIENCE ▼

Bean Trauma (up to 5 minutes) After everyone has arrived, have students form a circle. Give each student one of the soil-filled paper cups you prepared. Say: **Without spilling any dirt, find the bean in your cup. Once you've found the bean, destroy it.**

After kids have finished, collect the paper cups. Then have kids form foursomes to discuss these questions:
● **Did you just commit "plant murder"? Why or why not?**
● **How was this experience like human abortion? How was it different?**
● **Do you think abortion is murder? Why or why not?**
● **How did your attempts to destroy the bean affect the other contents of the cup?**
● **How was this activity like how one family member's involvement in an abortion would affect the whole family? How is it different?**

Say: **Just as the soil was affected by removing the bean in our experiment, family members are affected by abortion. That's one reason it's so important for us to talk about abortion. Today we're going to discuss various views about abortion and explore abortion's effect on families because your family is important to God.**

LEADER TIP for The Study

Whenever you ask groups to discuss a list of questions, write the questions on newsprint, and tape the newsprint to a space on a wall that's designated as the "Question Area." Then groups can discuss the questions at their own pace.

CREATIVE DISCUSSION ▼

Anonymous Debate (20 to 25 minutes) Say: **As we discuss the issues surrounding abortion, we need to remember one very important thing: We need to act and speak lovingly and respectfully toward each other. To help us do this, we're going to conduct a very different kind of debate.**

Before beginning the debate, have foursomes pray together, asking God to teach them his views on abortion and families. Also encourage students to ask God to help them discuss this emotional subject in a spirit of love.

When foursomes have finished praying, hand each student an index card and a pencil. On their cards, have kids write their opinions about abortion then place their cards in a paper bag. Pass the bag around the room, and have each student draw out a card. For the remainder of the debate, everyone must discuss the abortion issue from the perspective

Rock-a-Bye Baby   38

written on his or her card.

Say: **Read the opinions about abortion posted on the walls, and then decide which opinion is most similar to the opinion on your card. When you've made a decision, stand in the appropriate section of the room as marked by the tape on the floor.**

After everyone has chosen an area to stand in, distribute copies of the "Questions List" handout (p. 44), and have kids in each area discuss the first question under their section's opinion heading.

After a minute of discussion, say: **If you believe the arguments you've just heard are strong enough, you can "change" the opinion on your card and move to an area in the room that better reflects the new opinion.**

After kids move to a new opinion area, have them continue the discussion using the questions listed under their new opinion heading. After each question, invite kids to reassess the opinion on the card and to move to an opinion area that more adequately reflects their views. Continue until kids have discussed five questions. Then ask:

● **How did these questions involve other members of the pregnant person's family?**

● **How well does the opinion you're standing by consider others in the mother's family? in the father's family? in both parents' future families?**

● **Does the opinion you're standing by seem to consider that your family is important to God? Explain.**

Then say: **Now that you've clarified the point of view written on your card, let's explore Scripture to seek God's view of abortion, looking for understanding of how your family is important to God.**

> **LEADER TIP for Anonymous Debate**
>
> When your students first choose an opinion area, they may all end up in the same area. If this happens, begin the discussion with the class as it is, or invite kids to spread themselves among the other opinion areas for a more diverse debate.

BIBLE EXPLORATION ▼

Seeking God's View (15 to 20 minutes)

Have students form groups of four, and distribute Bibles, pencils, and paper to each group. In each group, have kids choose two readers to read the Bible passages, a recorder to keep notes of the discussion, and a reporter to tell the class about the group's discussion. In their groups, have kids read Genesis 2:18-24 and then discuss these questions:

● **What does this Scripture say about family?**

● **Does this Scripture add anything to our discussion about abortion? Explain.**

Have reporters from each group summarize the group's discussion for the class. Then have groups read Exodus 21:22-25 and discuss these questions:

● **What does this Scripture say about the value of an unborn child's life? of the mother's life?**

● **What does this Scripture say about family?**

● **Does this Scripture add anything to our discussion about abortion? Explain.**

Leader TIP for Seeking God's View

Some people think Exodus 21:22-25 demands justice for injury to a baby. Other people think this Scripture demands justice for injury to a pregnant woman.

Some groups point to this Scripture to condone acts of violence directed toward abortion providers or women who have had abortions. Other groups point to this Scripture as evidence that God esteems a woman's life over a baby's life. We've included this Scripture because it is used to support very different opinions about abortion. However, you may want to discuss the Scripture more fully with your kids, emphasizing that Christ changed Old Testament law from "eye for eye" to "turn the other cheek" (Matthew 5:38-42).

Have reporters from each group summarize the group's discussion for the class. Then have groups read Psalm 139:13-16 and Jeremiah 1:4-5 and discuss these questions:

● **Since God knew and had plans for King David and the prophet Jeremiah before they were born, do you think God knew you before you were born? Explain.**

● **Do you think God knows all babies before they are born? Explain.**

● **What does this Scripture say about family?**

● **Does this Scripture add anything to our discussion about abortion? Explain.**

Have reporters from each group summarize the group's discussion. Then have groups read 1 Timothy 5:3-8 and discuss these questions:

● **What does this Scripture say is pleasing to God?**

● **What does this Scripture say about the importance of family members?**

● **What does this Scripture say about how we affect our families?**

● **Does this Scripture add anything to our discussion about abortion? Explain.**

Have reporters from each group summarize the group's discussion. Then ask groups to consider all the passages while they discuss these questions:

● **What do these passages say about God's view of family?**

● **What do they say about God's view of abortion?**

● **Based on Scripture, how does abortion affect your family?**

● **How can you use these passages to help you decide what to think about abortion?**

When kids have finished discussing the questions, have the groups decide which opinion area from the previous activity best represents what the Scriptures say about abortion. Have the whole group stand in that opinion area. Then have each reporter explain to the class why the group chose to stand in that opinion area.

Say: **As we can see from the Bible passages we just explored, your family is important to God. Based on this truth, what will you choose to believe about abortion?**

RESPONSE AND COMMITMENT ▼

True Stories (10 to 15 minutes) Have kids stay with their groups. Ask two volunteers to each read aloud one of the following Bible passages: Psalm 130:1-4 and Ephesians 4:29-32. Then say: **God wants to forgive us whenever we make sinful choices, and he wants us to show love and forgiveness to others.**

To add a human touch to today's study, you'll hear four quotes from teenage girls that were posted on an America Online message board about teenage pregnancy. Based on what you've learned about abortion, the family, and forgiveness, think about

Rock-a-Bye Baby 40

how you'd like to respond to these girls. Ask four volunteers to read aloud the following quotes:

● "I was pregnant at 15 and I decided to have an abortion. It was the best way to deal with it, in my opinion."

● "I got pregnant at 15 and had an abortion. It was the hardest and most painful thing I have ever done. To this day two years later it still makes me cry."

● "Once I decided to keep [the baby] my mother and father had different responses. My mother was 100 percent supportive, my father was about 90 percent because he thought the baby was going to hold me back from my dreams. But now they are both more excited than I sometimes am. They walk around telling folks that they are going to be grandparents."

● "My mom works for an adoption agency and a lot of these kids have a much better life after they were adopted. Not to say that anyone couldn't take care of their child, but with adoption you could give your child things that you couldn't if you had kept him/her…It's much better than abortion, in my opinion."

Have groups discuss these questions:

● **What's your reaction to these quotes?**

● **How do you think God feels about these quotes? about these girls?**

● **Which of these quotes best reflects the idea that your family is important to God?**

Distribute paper and pencils as you say: **Now think about how**

DEPTH FINDER — UNDERSTANDING THE ABORTION DEBATE

The debate about abortion rages in this country. Some claim that a woman has a right to her own body and to her privacy. Others picket abortion centers. Some even murder abortion doctors, claiming they're in a war for the lives of innocent children.

But what does God think? What's his stance on everything that surrounds the abortion issue?

The Bible doesn't specifically address all these subplots in the abortion debate, but it does describe God as the creator and giver of life. God created the heavens, the earth, and both animal and human life (Genesis 1–2). He also promised to create a new heaven and earth (Revelation 21:1-5). Jesus came to give abundant life to all who are "born again" (John 3:3-7; 10:10).

In direct opposition to God's love for life is Satan's lust for death. Where Jesus wants to give us life in all its fullness, Satan comes to "steal and kill and destroy" (John 10:10). Satan will do anything he can to separate us from God, the creator and giver of life, and that means he will encourage us to die any way we can—emotionally, physically, and most of all, spiritually.

So with these ideas in mind, what do you think God thinks about abortion? about picketing abortion clinics? about crisis-pregnancy clinics? about murdering doctors who perform abortions?

And how do God's thoughts impact your beliefs and actions?

LEADER TIP for The Study

WARNING! Students in your group may have had abortions or may have encouraged girlfriends to have abortions. This topic will be especially difficult for these young people. If you notice that a student is uncharacteristically quiet or more extroverted than usual, gently approach that person, talk about how he or she feels, and be prepared to refer the student to someone, such as a counselor or pastor, who can help the student process his or her feelings.

you'd like to respond to these girls if you read these quotes on the Internet. Write a message to any one or all of the girls about abortion or about how important their families are to God. Keep in mind what you've learned today about abortion, the family, and forgiveness. You have a couple of minutes to write a response to whomever you'd like.

After a couple of minutes, say: **Today's study may have brought up some tough issues for you. Perhaps you need to re-evaluate your views on abortion. Perhaps you know someone who's pregnant, and you need to help that person make a wise choice. Or maybe you have had an abortion or have encouraged someone to get one. Use this time of solitude to pray about these things. If you have something to confess to God, he will forgive you and restore life to you.**

When kids have finished praying, say: **Think about a commitment you can make this week about today's topic. Perhaps you can read more in the Bible about God's view of abortion. Or maybe you can organize a team of friends to gather donated baby clothes for a local crisis-pregnancy center. Or maybe you've had an abortion or know someone who's had an abortion and can pray about how that choice affected you, your family, and God.**

Before you dismiss the class, have kids write down their commitments on their papers. Tell kids to take their papers home as reminders of their commitments and of what they learned in class. Invite kids to talk with you after class; some may have related issues or concerns that they need to pray about with you.

"**My frame** was not hidden from you when I was made in the secret place. When I was woven together in the depths of the earth, your eyes saw my **unformed body.**"

—Psalm 139:15-16

DEPTH FINDER — UNDERSTANDING THESE KIDS

According to the Alan Guttmacher Institute, Planned Parenthood's research arm, 70 percent of women who have experienced abortions affiliate themselves with a church. Twenty-seven percent claim to attend church once a week. The institute concludes from these statistics that one in six women in church have had abortions (Sydna A. Massé, "Abortion: A Tough Reality in the World, the Church and the Parsonage," Pastor to Pastor newsletter, Oct. 1995).

So how many of them attend your youth group or Sunday school?

You may never know. Many girls, fearing the judgment and humiliation of going to church unwed and pregnant, choose abortion.

But these girls probably didn't make their decisions alone. After conducting interviews with a number of post-abortive women, Frederica Mathewes-Green made the following observation: "In nearly every case, the abortion was undertaken to fulfill a felt obligation to another person: a parent (and then, most often, her mother) or the father of her unborn child. The predictable barriers of housing, jobs, and money faded rapidly in significance when these women were faced with a loved one's disapproving frown" ("Why Women Choose Abortion," Christianity Today magazine, Jan. 9, 1995).

The results of Mathewes-Green's interviews point toward something that you, as a youth leader, can do to help the young people in your group avoid having abortions: Build supportive relationships with them, and find other adults who will do the same. Your young women need to know that if they become pregnant, they have a wise adult who will listen to them and will help them without judging them. They need to know that if they go against the wishes of parents or boyfriends by choosing to keep their babies, someone will walk through their pregnancies with them.

So speak sensitively to your students about teen pregnancy and abortion. Teach your kids the truth about premarital sex and abortion, but also remind them that God loves them and will forgive them for every sin they ever commit.

LEADER TIP for The Study

If one of your students tells you that she's pregnant or that he has gotten someone pregnant, she or he will need help making tough decisions. Consider referring this student to a Care Net program or service. Care Net is a nonprofit, Christian, pro-life network of pregnancy care centers and churches that approaches unanticipated pregnancies nonjudgmentally and nonpolitically.

To find the Care Net programs or services near you, contact Care Net at

109 Carpenter Drive #100
Sterling, VA 20164
phone: (703) 478-5661
fax: (703) 478-5668
e-mail: etlanna@ix.net com.com
Web site: www.goshen.net/CareNet

Not only do many of Care Net's services help people through crisis pregnancies, but they also provide post-abortion counseling.

QUESTIONS LIST

Opinion Area 1: Abortion is murder. It's always wrong.

DISCUSSION QUESTIONS: What about in cases of rape? What about when the mother's life is in danger? What about in cases of incest? What if the parents knew the child would be horribly deformed? If the embryo can't live on its own, how can you prove that it's a separate human life?

Opinion Area 2: Abortion should be legal and free for everyone.

DISCUSSION QUESTIONS: What about the people who would use abortion as a free form of birth control? Why should my tax dollars be used to pay for someone's abortion—especially if I think abortion is morally wrong? Why should abortion be free when so many other lifesaving medical procedures aren't? How is making abortion free and legal any different from making murder free and legal? How is abortion any less murderous than assisted suicide?

Opinion Area 3: Abortion is private. It should be legal but not paid for by the government.

DISCUSSION QUESTIONS: How can you say murder is a private issue? What about the rights of the father or the grandparents to help decide whether an abortion is the best answer? By keeping abortion "private," aren't you putting way too much power into the hands of just one person? What about people who can't afford an abortion—shouldn't the government help them? What kind of democracy would this be if only the rich could have abortions?

Opinion Area 4: Abortion is OK as long as a girl's parents give their permission.

DISCUSSION QUESTIONS: What about parents who don't have their child's best interests at heart? What about kids who don't live at home? How can you decide at what age it's suddenly OK for women to decide on abortion for themselves? Why should parents have the right to tell their child what to do with her own body? What about the father's or the father's parents' right to decide what happens to the baby?

Opinion Area 5: Abortion is OK only in cases of rape or when the mother's life is at stake.

DISCUSSION QUESTIONS: How can you dictate what's right or wrong for someone else? What gives you the right to force a child to come into the world when you'll have absolutely no responsibility in raising it? What about pregnant women caught in deep poverty—how can you deny them the right to an abortion? Why should we allow the government to dictate morality to us? If we allow the government to dictate morality on the issue of abortion, what's to stop it from making laws on other moral issues that we may disagree with?

Permission to photocopy this handout from Group's Core Belief Bible Study Series granted for local church use.
Copyright © Group Publishing, Inc., P.O. Box 481, Loveland, CO 80539.

THE ISSUE: Siblings

Why Can't We Just Get Along?
Helping Kids Love Their Siblings

by Erin McKay

■ It's a problem the very first family faced: Siblings have a tough time getting along. ■ You don't have to get very far into the Bible to find siblings who definitely were not the best of friends. Even when sibling rivalry was not expressed violently (as it was in the story of Cain and Abel in Genesis 4), it certainly caused discord. ■ Unfortunately, not a lot has changed. Kids still struggle with their siblings. ■ Much the way brothers and sisters in the Bible treated each other, siblings today often take each other for granted, fail to be considerate, and look to place blame. When talking about their siblings, kids frequently complain about such issues as dishonesty during play, name-calling, disregard for privacy and personal property, and competition for attention. ■ In contrast to the behavior just described, the Bible encourages us to "keep on loving each other as brothers" (Hebrews 13:1), implying that love between siblings should be the model for love between people in general and believers in particular. ■ But do your teenagers understand what that kind of love looks like? ■ In this study, kids will experience empathy, negotiation, teamwork, and appreciation. They'll discover that empathizing leads to negotiation, which fosters teamwork, which generates a feeling of appreciation for others. Through these experiences, kids will learn about brotherly love and will realize that despite differences, brothers and sisters can be friends.

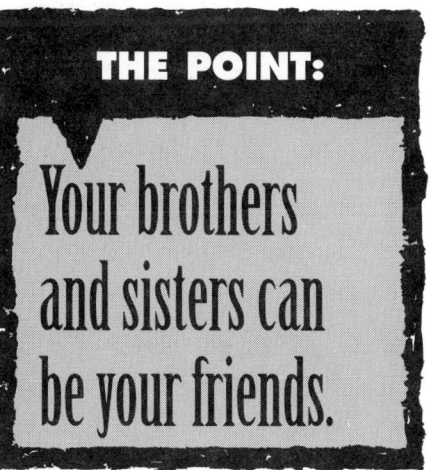

THE POINT:

Your brothers and sisters can be your friends.

The Study AT A GLANCE

SECTION	MINUTES	WHAT STUDENTS WILL DO	SUPPLIES
Empathy Exercise	10 to 15	BEST (DRESSED) FOOT FORWARD—Learn about empathy by participating in a relay race wearing unusual footwear.	Bibles, footwear as described in the "Before the Study" box (p. 47), masking tape, marker, clean socks, suitcase or bag, paper scraps, small bag or box
Negotiation Investigation	25 to 30	SIBLING SCENARIOS—Create presentations depicting conflicts between siblings, see the conflicts from each sibling's viewpoint, and then practice negotiating solutions.	Bibles, "Sibling Scenarios" handouts (pp. 54-55), scissors, newsprint, marker, tape
Teamwork Training	10 to 15	THE TIES THAT BIND—Use teamwork to mentally and physically meet a challenge.	Rolls of crepe paper, two rolls of tape
Appreciation Application	up to 5	FINDING FRIENDS—Acknowledge traits in one another that are desirable in friends and realize that siblings often have these same traits.	Tape, newsprint, marker, "Friendship Bracelets" handouts (p. 56), pens, transparent tape, scissors

notes:

THE POINT OF "WHY CAN'T WE JUST GET ALONG?":

Your brothers and sisters can be your friends.

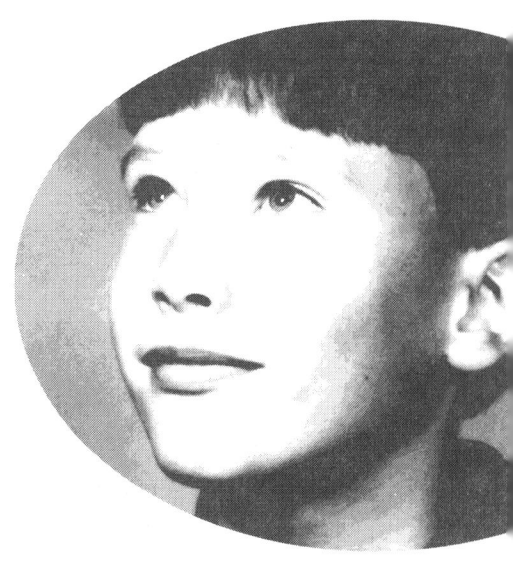

THE BIBLE CONNECTION

GENESIS 37:17b-28; **NUMBERS 12:1-9;** and **LUKE 10:38-42**	Conflict arises between brothers and sisters.
MATTHEW 5:23-24; **18:15, 21-22;** **EPHESIANS 4:1-3;** **1 PETER 3:8-9;** and **1 JOHN 4:19-21**	Our conduct toward others should be loving.
MATTHEW 12:46-50	Jesus compares his followers to brothers and sisters.
HEBREWS 13:1	We're to treat each other as brothers.

In this study, kids will experience empathy through a relay race, act out sibling disputes to learn about negotiation, use teamwork to solve a challenge, and appreciate friendly qualities in one another.

Through these activities, kids can learn to respect their siblings' viewpoints, to lovingly resolve differences, to see qualities in their siblings that they look for in friends, and even to enjoy their siblings.

BEFORE THE STUDY

For the "Best (Dressed) Foot Forward" activity, gather several different pieces of footwear such as a tennis shoe, a ballet slipper and a beach flipper (in an equal number of right and left shoes). On the bottom of each shoe, affix a piece of masking tape with a number written on it. For example, label the tennis shoe with a "1," the ballet slipper with a "2," and so on. Put the shoes and some clean socks into a suitcase or bag. Also, write the same numbers on scraps of paper, and put the scraps into a small bag.

Then photocopy the "Sibling Scenarios" handout (pp. 54-55), and cut the handout into separate scenarios. You'll also need to write the following Scripture references on a piece of newsprint and tape the newsprint to a wall: Matthew 5:23-24; Matthew 18:15; Matthew 18:21-22; Ephesians 4:1-3; 1 Peter 3:8-9; and 1 John 4:19-21.

Photocopy the "Friendship Bracelets" handout (p. 56) onto colorful paper, and cut apart the bracelet strips. Make sure you have one bracelet strip for each person.

LEADER TIP

for Best (Dressed) Foot Forward

The number of shoes you'll need depends on how many teams you'll use during the "Best (Dressed) Foot Forward" activity. You'll need only two shoes for each team, so if you have fewer than fifteen kids in your group, you'll need four shoes.

Why Can't We Just Get Along? 47

THE STUDY

EMPATHY EXERCISE ▼

Best (Dressed) Foot Forward (10 to 15 minutes)

After everyone has arrived, ask:
- How many of you have brothers or sisters?
- What do you like about having brothers and sisters?
- What do you dislike about having brothers and sisters?

Say: **Most of us struggle to some degree with our brothers and sisters. But we can learn a lot about how to treat other people through our relationships with our brothers and sisters.**

Ask volunteers to read aloud Matthew 12:46-50 and Hebrews 13:1. Ask:
- Who do these Scriptures say our brothers and sisters are?
- Why do you think we're to treat each other "as brothers"?
- If the Bible says we're to treat each other "as brothers," and if Jesus called believers his brothers and sisters, how do you think God feels about the relationship between brothers and sisters?

Say: **We may have brothers and sisters at home. Or we may have brothers and sisters in Christ. Regardless, we need to treat all our brothers and sisters the way God wants us to. So today we're going to learn about some tools to help us get along with our siblings. Let's find out how your brothers and sisters can be your friends.**

Have kids form two teams and line up single file with their teammates at one end of the room. Put the suitcase of shoes and socks between the teams. Then have the first two people from each team choose two numbers from the small bag. Have those students find the corresponding shoes in the suitcase and then return to their teams.

Explain to kids that they will be participating in a relay in which they

LEADER TIP for Best (Dressed) Foot Forward

If you have more than fourteen students, you may want to have kids form additional teams. Just be sure to provide two shoes for each team.

LEADER TIP for Best (Dressed) Foot Forward

You may want to allow team members to swap numbers so that each team has a right shoe and a left shoe.

LEADER TIP for The Study

Whenever groups discuss a list of questions, write the list on newsprint, and tape it to a wall so groups can discuss the questions at their own pace.

DEPTH FINDER — UNDERSTANDING THE BIBLE

While specific instructions regarding sibling relationships seem difficult to find in the Bible, many passages suggest that God wants families to provide centers of love and support from which members "fan out" to do his work. The first two words of the Lord's Prayer in Matthew 6:9b, "Our Father," and passages such as Matthew 12:46-50; Galatians 3:26-28; and Ephesians 4:4-6 tell us that Christians are all brothers and sisters in a figurative sense.

Although squabbles between siblings seem to be a fact of family life, brothers and sisters can be friends when empathy, negotiation, teamwork, and appreciation are encouraged.

DEPTH FINDER: UNDERSTANDING THE IMPORTANCE OF SIBLING RELATIONSHIPS

The opinion that families are crucial to the well-being of individuals and society is widely held. Here are some examples:

● "The Bible speaks of the family as the strategic contact point between the individual and the larger community. The family is a buffer, offering refuge and peace...It is an environment for developing relationships...meeting needs...and communicating ideas" (David S. Dockery et al., eds., *Holman Bible Handbook*).

● "The interaction that we have with our siblings during childhood can deeply affect our feelings of self-esteem and help us develop social skills that will carry us through the rest of our lives. We learn how to comfort and empathize with another person, how to make jokes, resolve arguments, even how to irritate one another. All the things we learn with and from our siblings we use later in life" (Mark Victor Hansen and Barbara Nichols, *Out of the Blue*).

● "Children's relationships with their siblings have a major impact on their social outlook...The relationships children develop with their brothers and sisters will, as they grow, influence their ability to read other people's emotions" (Beth Azar, APA Monitor, from the American Psychological Association's Web site).

Help your kids understand the importance of learning to get along with their siblings; it'll set them straight on healthy relationships for life.

have to put on their teams' shoes, *walk*—not run—to the other end of the room and back, and then hand the shoes to the next person in line. Tell kids that the relay will continue until everyone has had a chance to walk across the room and back.

Allow kids to borrow a pair of socks from the suitcase, give them time to put the socks on, and then begin the relay. After the relay, ask:

● **Was it easy or difficult to walk in someone else's shoes? Why?**
● **What does it mean to "walk a mile in someone else's shoes"?**
● **Is it usually easy or difficult to see a situation from someone else's viewpoint? Why?**
● **When dealing with your brothers and sisters, do you usually see situations from their viewpoint? Explain.**
● **How do you think your relationships with your siblings would be affected if you tried to see things from their viewpoint?**

Say: **Even though you might not get along with your siblings all the time, <u>your brothers and sisters can be your friends</u>—especially if you learn to see things from your siblings' viewpoints. Let's look at some specific situations to see how that can work.**

LEADER TIP for The Study
Throughout the study, remind kids who don't have brothers and sisters at home that they can learn from the study how to treat their brothers and sisters in Christ.

NEGOTIATION INVESTIGATION ▼

Sibling Scenarios (25 to 30 minutes)
Have kids form six groups, and give each group a different scenario from the "Sibling Scenarios" handout (pp. 54-55). Explain that groups will have a few minutes to read their scenarios and

LEADER TIP for Sibling Scenarios
For this activity, each group should have between two and six participants. Duplicate or subtract scenarios as needed to accommodate the number of kids in your group.

Why Can't We Just Get Along? 49

create a presentation. Say: **In your presentations, you'll first need to summarize the conflict between the siblings in your scenario. You'll then need to present each sibling's viewpoint. Your group can be as creative as it wants to be to present this material, but everyone has to participate.**

Give groups about five minutes to prepare, and then have each group take a turn presenting its scenario. Lead kids in applauding each group's efforts. After all the groups have presented, ask:

● **What problems were the siblings in these scenarios facing?**

● **When you heard the different viewpoints, did your feelings or opinions about the conflict change? Why or why not?**

● **If the people in these scenarios could see things from their siblings' viewpoints, do you think they could work out their problems? Why or why not?**

Say: **Each of us has felt jealousy, envy, or resentment toward others. Although it's natural to feel anger toward our siblings from time to time, the Bible tells us how we should treat our brothers and sisters.**

From the newsprint you prepared before the study, assign each group two Scriptures. Say: **Your group will have another few minutes to read your Scriptures and create a new presentation. This time, you'll first need to summarize in your own words what the Scriptures tell us about how we should treat each other. You'll then need to present how the siblings in your scenario could negotiate a solution to their conflict if they considered each other's viewpoints and the principles from the Scriptures. Again, your group can be as creative as it wants to be to present this material as long as everyone participates.**

Give groups about five minutes to prepare, and then have each group take a turn presenting its solutions. Lead kids in applauding each

---

DEPTH FINDER — ALL IN THE FAMILY

Sadly, many biblical disputes between siblings stem from selfishness, jealousy, or resentment. Here are some examples:

● Genesis 37 records the betrayal of Joseph at the hands of his brothers, who were jealous that Joseph was their father's favorite son.

● In Numbers 12:1-9, Aaron and Miriam complained about their brother Moses' wife. The Quest Study Bible states that Miriam and Aaron were jealous of Moses' position as God's spokesperson; they expressed their jealousy by criticizing Moses' wife.

● In the story about Mary and Martha recorded in Luke 10:38-42, Jesus chastises Martha for not recognizing what is truly important (listening to him) and for being more concerned about the equitable distribution of work.

● In *The Bible in Time*, Stephen Travis points out that the brother in Jesus' parable of the prodigal son (Luke 15:11-31) was "out of step with the generosity of God."

Modern siblings, who are just as vocal about supposed inequities, can learn a lot from their biblical counterparts. In each of the examples just described, siblings received or extended forgiveness to overcome differences and better serve God.

group's efforts. After all the groups have presented, ask:

● **From these presentations, what did you learn about how we should treat our brothers and sisters?**

● **What did you have to do to negotiate solutions?**

● **When the siblings considered each other's viewpoints as well as the principles in the Scriptures, how well were they able to negotiate solutions? Explain.**

● **If you used these guidelines with your brothers and sisters, what difference would it make? Explain.**

● **Why is it sometimes difficult to follow these guidelines?**

● **What do you think you should do if your siblings don't treat you according to these guidelines? Why?**

Say: **It's important to understand that you can disagree with people and still love them. If we focus on Christ, though, we can be at peace with one another. And when we try to see things from someone else's viewpoint, we're better able to negotiate good solutions to problems. And when we're willing to negotiate, we're one step closer to realizing that** <u>our brothers and sisters can be our friends</u>**. Now let's practice the next step.**

TEAMWORK TRAINING ▼

The Ties That Bind (10 to 15 minutes) Have kids help you clear furniture from one area of the room. Then have kids re-form the groups they were in for the opening relay and stand in lines with their groups. Say: **Imagine that your group is a caterpillar. I'm going to give the first person in each line a roll of crepe paper and a roll of tape, and each group has to figure out how to spin itself into a cocoon. There are only two rules. First, except for the lead person in each group, you must keep at least one hand on the shoulder of the person in front of you at all times. In other words, you must always stay "connected." Second, you may talk to each other, but you may not watch the other group. Ready? You've got about five minutes to spin your cocoons!** Hand each lead person a roll of crepe paper and a roll of tape, and have groups begin.

After this activity, have kids "emerge" from their cocoons and gather crepe paper to be used again or discarded. Then ask:

● **What was it like to be connected to each other during this activity?**

● **What was easy or difficult about completing the task while you were all connected?**

● **How did working with others affect your caterpillar?**

● **What can make a team work well?**

● **Did teamwork help you negotiate any of the problems between siblings in the scenarios you presented earlier? How?**

● **Can anyone describe an occasion when you and a sibling had fun together even though you were "working" on something?**

● **How could you apply what you learned in accomplishing this**

LEADER TIP for The Ties That Bind

Kids might come up with many different ways to solve this "puzzle." For example, if the lead person tapes one end of the crepe paper to a chair and starts stretching the paper around the perimeter of a group of chairs (with the rest of his or her teammates following), the caterpillar can curl around inside the cocoon. Or a group might form a big circle and pass the roll of crepe paper from person to person (on the outside) so that it winds around the caterpillar.

challenge to working together with your brothers and sisters?

Say: **Because every person—even brothers and sisters—has strengths and gifts to share, we work best when we work together.**

So far you've learned that when you try to see things from your siblings' viewpoints, you can negotiate good solutions to problems. And when you negotiate good solutions, you find that your brothers and sisters actually make good teammates. And all that helps you to realize that <u>your brothers and sisters can be your friends</u>.

APPRECIATION APPLICATION ▼

Finding Friends (up to 5 minutes) Tape a sheet of newsprint to a wall, and then ask kids to call out qualities they look for or appreciate in friends.

Have kids form pairs, and give everyone a pen and a bracelet strip from the "Friendship Bracelets" handout (p. 56). Ask each student to write on his or her bracelet a quality of a good friend that also describes his or her partner. Then have kids exchange bracelets, and pass around tape for kids to use to fasten their bracelets.

Say: **If any of you has a brother or sister at home, raise your hand and keep it raised. If any of you has a brother or sister "in Christ," raise your hand also.**

Take a look around the room at all of us who are siblings. Each of us has qualities that people look for in friends. Have kids look at the newsprint list of qualities they look for or appreciate in friends. Ask:

● **Which of these qualities do your brothers and sisters have?**

DEPTHFINDER — LOVE 'EM OR LEAVE 'EM?

Some kids (as well as adults) are puzzled at the seeming detachment from immediate family that Jesus expressed on a number of occasions (Matthew 10:34-39; Matthew 12:46-50; and Matthew 19:29).

In *All the Apostles of the Bible*, Herbert Lockyer offers one possible explanation: "As for Zebedee...father of James and John, he appears only in the gospel narrative on the occasion when his sons left him to follow Jesus. Either he died shortly after they had entered on their discipleship, or, what is more probable, as an orthodox Jew, he did not share their faith in Jesus, nor approve of the discipleship they had chosen. One wonders whether Jesus had Zebedee and his opposition in mind when He spoke about forsaking father and mother for His sake."

It's also possible that Jesus was warning against a "clan" kind of mentality, so that our love for others might be more all-inclusive. In addition, many people believe Jesus was emphasizing the importance of having a stronger allegiance to God than to anything or anyone else—even family.

● What qualities do your brothers and sisters have that *you* look for in friends?

Say: **Just as your brothers and sisters have friends outside the family, <u>your brothers and sisters can be your friends</u>.**

Today we've talked about learning to see our siblings' viewpoints, negotiating with them, practicing teamwork, and appreciating their good qualities. This week, remember that <u>your brothers and sisters can be your friends</u>, and try to use what you've learned today to be good friends to them.

To close, pray these words from Stephen Travis' *The Bible in Time:* "Lord, enable me today to love rather than to retaliate, to encourage rather than to criticize, so that I may be not merely a hearer but a doer of your life-giving word." Amen.

"Finally, all of you, live in → HARMONY with one another; be sympathetic, love as brothers, be compassionate and humble. Do not repay evil with evil or insult with insult, but with blessing."

—1 Peter 3:8-9a

Why Can't We Just Get Along?

SIBLING scenarios

SCENARIO 1: Genesis 37:17b-28

When Joseph was a boy, he was his father's favorite son. Joseph's brothers were so jealous of him that they sold him as a slave to some Egyptians.

Many years later, Joseph found himself in a position to either destroy or save his brothers. Because of a famine, Joseph's brothers went to Egypt to buy food. Joseph was then a governor of Egypt and had the power to either save his brothers or turn them away.

- Summarize the conflict between Joseph and his brothers.
- Present both Joseph's and the brothers' viewpoints as if they are explaining to someone how they felt and why they acted the way they did.

SCENARIO 2: Numbers 12:1-9

Miriam and Aaron were jealous of their brother Moses because he was God's spokesperson to the entire nation of Israel. They dealt with their feelings by complaining about Moses' wife, who was a foreigner.

God was not pleased with their behavior, and he gathered Moses, Miriam, and Aaron together to reprimand Miriam and Aaron. When God had finished talking, Miriam was suddenly sick with leprosy.

- Summarize the conflict between Miriam, Aaron, and Moses.
- Present Miriam's, Aaron's, and Moses' viewpoints as if they are explaining to someone how they felt and why they acted the way they did.

SCENARIO 3: Luke 10:38-42

Jesus taught in the home of two sisters, Mary and Martha. Mary sat, listening to Jesus, while Martha cleaned the home and prepared a meal. Exasperated, Martha complained to Jesus that Mary wasn't helping her and asked Jesus to chastise Mary.

- Summarize the conflict between Mary and Martha.
- Present both Mary's and Martha's viewpoints as if they are explaining to someone how they felt and why they acted the way they did.

Permission to photocopy this handout from Group's Core Belief Bible Study Series granted for local church use.
Copyright © Group Publishing, Inc., P.O. Box 481, Loveland, CO 80539.

scenario 4

Bill was building a model airplane when Diane walked into the room. Although the television was on, Bill didn't appear to be watching it, so Diane changed the channel. Bill got mad, and they started arguing about who should be able to watch what.

- Summarize the conflict between Bill and Diane.
- Present both Bill's and Diane's viewpoints as if they are explaining to someone how they felt and why they acted the way they did.

scenario 5

Jennifer's youth group was going bowling one evening, and she couldn't decide what to wear. She decided to borrow Tracy's blouse—without asking. Several hours later, Tracy frantically searched for her blouse while getting ready to go out with friends. She ended up putting on another outfit she didn't like nearly as much; then she saw Jennifer heading out the door in her blouse. They began to argue.

- Summarize the conflict between Jennifer and Tracy.
- Present both Jennifer's and Tracy's viewpoints as if they are explaining to someone how they felt and why they acted the way they did.

scenario 6

Kevin and Jed are responsible for chores around the house such as cleaning the kitty-litter box and mowing the yard. On Tuesday night, their mom asked whether the trash had been taken outside for collection the next morning. Kevin and Jed couldn't agree on whose turn it was to take out the trash.

- Summarize the conflict between Kevin and Jed.
- Present both Kevin's and Jed's viewpoints as if they are explaining to someone how they felt and why they acted the way they did.

Friendship Bracelets

BROTHERS and SISTERS can be friends.

BROTHERS and SISTERS can be friends.

BROTHERS and SISTERS can be friends.

BROTHERS and SISTERS can be friends.

BROTHERS and SISTERS can be friends.

BROTHERS and SISTERS can be friends.

BROTHERS and SISTERS can be friends.

BROTHERS and SISTERS can be friends.

BROTHERS and SISTERS can be friends.

BROTHERS and SISTERS can be friends.

why ▼ Active and Interactive Learning works with teenagers

Let's Start With the Big Picture

Think back to a major life lesson you've learned.
Got it? Now answer these questions:
- Did you learn your lesson from something you read?
- Did you learn it from something you heard?
- Did you learn it from something you experienced?

If you're like 99 percent of your peers, you answered "yes" only to the third question—you learned your life lesson from something you experienced.

This simple test illustrates the most convincing reason for using active and interactive learning with young people: People learn best through experience. Or to put it even more simply, people learn by doing.

Learning by doing is what active learning is all about. No more sitting quietly in chairs and listening to a speaker expound theories about God—that's passive learning. Active learning gets kids out of their chairs and into the experience of life. With active learning, kids get to *do* what they're studying. They *feel* the effects of the principles you teach. They *learn* by experiencing truth firsthand.

Active learning works because it recognizes three basic learning needs and uses them in concert to enable young people to make discoveries on their own and to find practical life applications for the truths they believe.

So what are these three basic learning needs?
1. Teenagers need action.
2. Teenagers need to think.
3. Teenagers need to talk.

Read on to find out exactly how these needs will be met by using the active and interactive learning techniques in Group's Core Belief Bible Study Series in your youth group.

1. Teenagers Need Action

Aircraft pilots know well the difference between passive and active learning. Their passive learning comes through listening to flight instructors and reading flight-instruction books. Their active learning comes through actually flying an airplane or flight simulator. Books and lectures may be helpful, but pilots really learn to fly by manipulating a plane's controls themselves.

We can help young people learn in a similar way. Though we may engage students passively in some reading and listening to teachers, their understanding and application of God's Word will really take off through simulated and real-life experiences.

Forms of active learning include simulation games; role-plays; service projects; experiments; research projects; group pantomimes; mock trials; construction projects; purposeful games; field trips; and, of course, the most powerful form of active learning—real-life experiences.

We can more fully explain active learning by exploring four of its characteristics:

● **Active learning is an adventure.** Passive learning is almost always predictable. Students sit passively while the teacher or speaker follows a planned outline or script.

In active learning, kids may learn lessons the teacher never envisioned. Because the leader trusts students to help create the learning experience, learners may venture into unforeseen discoveries. And often the teacher learns as much as the students.

● **Active learning is fun and captivating.** What are we communicating when we say, "OK, the fun's over—time to talk about God"? What's the hidden message? That joy is separate from God? And that learning is separate from joy?

What a shame.

Active learning is not joyless. One seventh-grader we interviewed clearly remembered her best Sunday school lesson: "Jesus was the light, and we went into a dark room and shut off the lights. We had a candle, and we learned that Jesus is the light and the dark can't shut off the light." That's active learning. Deena enjoyed the lesson. She had fun. And she learned.

Active learning intrigues people. Whether they find a foot-washing experience captivating or maybe a bit uncomfortable, they learn. And they learn on a level deeper than any work sheet or teacher's lecture could ever reach.

● **Active learning involves everyone.** Here the difference between passive and active learning becomes abundantly clear. It's like the difference between watching a football game on television and actually playing in the game.

The "trust walk" provides a good example of involving everyone in active learning. Half of the group members put on blindfolds; the other half serve as guides. The "blind" people trust the guides to lead them through the building or outdoors. The guides prevent the blind people from falling down stairs or tripping over rocks. Everyone needs to participate to learn the inherent lessons of trust, faith, doubt, fear, confidence, and servanthood. Passive spectators of this experience would learn little, but participants learn a great deal.

● **Active learning is focused through debriefing.** Activity simply for activity's sake doesn't usually result in good learning. Debriefing—evaluating an experience by discussing it in pairs or small groups—helps focus the experience and draw out its meaning. Debriefing helps sort and order the information students gather during the experience. It helps learners relate the recently experienced activity to their lives.

The process of debriefing is best started immediately after an experience. We use a three-step process in debriefing: reflection, interpretation, and application.

Reflection—This first step asks the students, "How did you feel?" Active-learning experiences typically evoke an emotional reaction, so it's appropriate to begin debriefing at that level.

Some people ask, "What do feelings have to do with education?" Feelings have everything to do with education. Think back again to that time in your life when you learned a big lesson. In all likelihood, strong feelings accompanied that lesson. Our emotions tend to cement things into our memories.

When you're debriefing, use open-ended questions to probe feelings. Avoid questions that can be answered with a "yes" or "no." Let your learners know that there are no wrong answers to these "feeling" questions. Everyone's feelings are valid.

Interpretation—The next step in the debriefing process asks, "What does this mean to you? How is this experience like or unlike some other aspect of your life?" Now you're asking people to identify a message or principle from the experience.

You want your learners to discover the message for themselves. So instead of telling students your answers, take the time to ask questions that encourage self-discovery. Use Scripture and discussion in pairs or small groups to explore how the actions and effects of the activity might translate to their lives.

Alert! Some of your people may interpret wonderful messages that you never intended. That's not failure! That's the Holy Spirit at work. God allows us to catch different glimpses of his kingdom even when we all look through the same glass.

Application—The final debriefing step asks, "What will you do about it?" This step moves learning into action. Your young people have shared a common experience. They've discovered a principle. Now they must create something new with what they've just experienced and interpreted. They must integrate the message into their lives.

The application stage of debriefing calls for a decision. Ask your students how they'll change, how they'll grow, what they'll do as a result of your time together.

2. Teenagers Need to Think

Today's students have been trained not to think. They aren't dumber than previous generations. We've simply conditioned them not to use their heads.

You see, we've trained our kids to respond with the simplistic answers they think the teacher wants to hear. Fill-in-the-blank student workbooks and teachers who ask dead-end questions such as "What's the capital of Delaware?" have produced kids and adults who have learned not to think.

And it doesn't just happen in junior high or high school. Our children are schooled very early not to think. Teachers attempt to help kids read with nonsensical fill-in-the-blank drills, word scrambles, and missing-letter puzzles.

Helping teenagers think requires a paradigm shift in how we teach. We need to plan for and set aside time for higher-order thinking and be willing to reduce our time spent on lower-order parroting. Group's Core Belief Bible Study Series is designed to help you do just that.

Thinking classrooms look quite different from traditional classrooms. In most church environments, the teacher does most of the talking and hopes that knowledge will transmit from his or her brain to the students'. In thinking settings, the teacher coaches students to ponder, wonder, imagine, and problem-solve.

3. Teenagers Need to Talk

Everyone knows that the person who learns the most in any class is the teacher. Explaining a concept to someone else is usually more helpful to the explainer than to the listener. So why not let the students do more teaching? That's one of the chief benefits of letting kids do the talking. This process is called interactive learning.

What is interactive learning? Interactive learning occurs when students discuss and work cooperatively in pairs or small groups.

Interactive learning encourages learners to work together. It honors the fact that students can learn from one another, not just from the teacher. Students work together in pairs or small groups to accomplish shared goals. They build together, discuss together, and present together. They teach each other and learn from one another. Success as a group is celebrated. Positive interdependence promotes individual and group learning.

Interactive learning not only helps people learn but also helps learners feel better about themselves and get along better with others. It accomplishes these things more effectively than the independent or competitive methods.

Here's a selection of interactive learning techniques that are used in Group's Core Belief Bible Study Series. With any of these models, leaders may assign students to specific partners or small groups. This will maximize cooperation and learning by preventing all the "rowdies" from linking up. And it will allow for new friendships to form outside of established cliques.

Following any period of partner or small-group work, the leader may reconvene the entire class for large-group processing. During this time the teacher may ask for reports or discoveries from individuals or teams. This technique builds in accountability for the teacherless pairs and small groups.

Pair-Share—With this technique each student turns to a partner and responds to a question or problem from the teacher or leader. Every learner responds. There are no passive observers. The teacher may then ask people to share their partners' responses.

Study Partners—Most curricula and most teachers call for Scripture passages to be read to the whole class by one person. One reads; the others doze.

Why not relinquish some teacher control and let partners read and react with each other? They'll all be involved—and will learn more.

Learning Groups—Students work together in small groups to create a model, design artwork, or study a passage or story; then they discuss what they learned through the experience. Each person in the learning group may be assigned a specific role. Here are some examples:

Reader

Recorder (makes notes of key thoughts expressed during the reading or discussion)

Checker (makes sure everyone understands and agrees with answers arrived at by the group)

Encourager (urges silent members to share their thoughts)

When everyone has a specific responsibility, knows what it is, and contributes to a small group, much is accomplished and much is learned.

Summary Partners—One student reads a paragraph, then the partner summarizes the paragraph or interprets its meaning. Partners alternate roles with each paragraph.

The paraphrasing technique also works well in discussions. Anyone who wishes to share a thought must first paraphrase what the previous person said. This sharpens listening skills and demonstrates the power of feedback communication.

Jigsaw—Each person in a small group examines a different concept, Scripture, or part of an issue. Then each teaches the others in the group. Thus, all members teach, and all must learn the others' discoveries. This technique is called a jigsaw because individuals are responsible to their group for different pieces of the puzzle.

JIGSAW EXAMPLE

Here's an example of a jigsaw.

Assign four-person teams. Have teammates each number off from one to four. Have all the Ones go to one corner of the room, all the Twos to another corner, and so on.

Tell team members they're responsible for learning information in their numbered corners and then for teaching their team members when they return to their original teams.

Give the following assignments to various groups:

Ones: Read Psalm 22. Discuss and list the prophecies made about Jesus.

Twos: Read Isaiah 52:13–53:12. Discuss and list the prophecies made about Jesus.

Threes: Read Matthew 27:1-32. Discuss and list the things that happened to Jesus.

Fours: Read Matthew 27:33-66. Discuss and list the things that happened to Jesus.

After the corner groups meet and discuss, instruct all learners to return to their original teams and report what they've learned. Then have each team determine which prophecies about Jesus were fulfilled in the passages from Matthew.

Call on various individuals in each team to report one or two prophecies that were fulfilled.

You Can Do It Too!

All this information may sound revolutionary to you, but it's really not. God has been using active and interactive learning to teach his people for generations. Just look at Abraham and Isaac, Jacob and Esau, Moses and the Israelites, Ruth and Boaz. And then there's Jesus, who used active learning all the time!

Group's Core Belief Bible Study Series makes it easy for you to use active and interactive learning with your group. The active and interactive elements are automatically built in! Just follow the outlines, and watch as your kids grow through experience and positive interaction with others.

FOR DEEPER STUDY

For more information on incorporating active and interactive learning into your work with teenagers, check out these resources:

- *Why Nobody Learns Much of Anything at Church: And How to Fix It*, by Thom and Joani Schultz (Group Publishing) and
- *Do It! Active Learning in Youth Ministry*, by Thom and Joani Schultz (Group Publishing).